# BERMONDSEY and ROTHERHITHE PERCEIVED

# BERMONDSEY and ROTHERHITHE PERCEIVED

Above: *The Bermondsey Street mural,* by Vincent Milne and Lynette Lombard; located on the wall of number four, Tanner St (at Bermondsey Street junction); it was executed in 1981 and was removed in 1998 (by then it had badly deteriorated). The turtle is (presumably) a reference to banner makers Turtle & Pearce, in Tanner Street. Other subjects depicted are (left to right): Monks and monastery, wine vaults, printing, docks, tanning and the leather trade, the first public laundry, 1977 Queen's Jubilee party, bonfire night, hop-picking and the antiques trade.

# BERMONDSEY

## and

## ROTHERHITHE

### PERCEIVED

A DESCRIPTIVE ACCOUNT OF TWO RIVERSIDE LOCALITIES,
WITH HISTORICAL NOTES AND ENGRAVINGS,
CONTEMPORARY PHOTOGRAPHS AND DRAWINGS

Compiled and written
by
Peter Marcan

LONDON:
PETER MARCAN PUBLICATIONS, 1998

Text © Peter Marcan, 1998

Published by: Peter Marcan Publications,
PO Box 3158, London SE1 4RA,
England, United Kingdom.
*Tel* (0171) 357 0368.

ISBN:  1 871811 14 7

First edition published 1992 under the title: *A Bermondsey and Rotherhithe Album.*
This edition should be retained as it contains some picture material and some text not included in this enlarged, revised, redesigned edition.

## COVER

Front cover shows: *The Navigators*, a sculpture made 1987 by David Kemp; located in Hays Galleria, near the riverside, this extraordinary creation weighs 15 tons, is made of steel and bronze, and its pumps and motors provide twenty kinetic and water features.

Back cover shows: *Mosaic mural at Swan Estate, Rotherhithe* (the oldest municipal housing in Rotherhithe, 1902-1903, between Rotherhithe Street and Brunel Road); executed by Bermondsey Artists' Group artists: David John, Steve Dunn, Jane Barnes, Frances Coleman, 1992.

## ACKNOWLEDGEMENTS/COPYRIGHT STATEMENT

The photographs of points of architectural and artistic interest and of buildings were commissioned from Lesley McDonald, who owns their copyright.

The following living artists have given me permission to reproduce their work, and they own its copyright:
Geoffrey Appleton, George Baker, Rose Cecil, Peter Chase, Martin Donlin, David Fried, Jonathan Huxley, Don Jarvis, David Lockett, John Vernon Lord, Martin Millard, Vincent Milne, Stephen Mumberson, Murals and Banners (Carol Kenna and Stephen Lobb), Jen Parker, Oscar Romp, Louise Soloway.
It has not proved possible to contact: Anthony Donaldson, Colin Kennedy, Peter Pelz. They are asked to contact the compiler/publisher should this publication come to their attention.

The following next of kin have authorised reproduction of work by deceased artists: The family of Nathaniel Kornbluth; Mrs Edna Williams (for Hubert Williams).
It has not proved possible to contact executors/next of kin for the following artists: R.J.Angel,
Joan Bloxam, Ernest Hasseldine, Sydney Robert Jones, William Washington. Anyone connected should contact the compiler/publisher.

## SBR, I; SBR II

These abbreviations are referred to as sources for relevant photographs:
SBR, I: Southwark, Bermondsey and Rotherhithe in old photographs. Alan Sutton, 1995.
SBR, II: Southwark, Bermondsey and Rotherhithe: a second selection. Sutton Publishing, 1997.
Both are compiled by Stephen Humphrey.

Printed by SRP Ltd, Exeter

# CONTENTS

# EARLY IMPRESSIONS OF BERMONDSEY

I crossed the river to Bermondsey to live there in 1991. I had longed for so long for a different environment, and for just a little more peacefulness. Here are some of my immediate impressions: a view on Bermondsey from a small bedsitter, overlooking a busy little side street:

Bermondsey is perhaps surprisingly a place of towers and turrets, of spires and extraordinary chimneys. Perhaps only from Bermondsey can you glimpse Tower Bridge looking so enticing, so magical. In Bermondsey Square the clinical precision of the tower block at Guy's Hospital on the horizon glares out at the tender gracefulness of St Mary's Church. In Tower Bridge Road the monumental chimney of Hartleys the old jam factory confronts the slender spire of Haddon Hall Baptist Church.

Bermondsey is also a place of boredom and anxiety, a place where many are unemployed, where so often there seems to be nothing at all to do; a place beneath the Thames at high tide, which feels too much like a backwater. In Bermondsey one must make daily attempts to find stimulation: gazing out of the window at the ever changing, variegated humanity, plunging into local newspapers, drinking strong black coffee, mad violin or piano playing sessions, writing letters to get letters back, reading, dreaming, trying to feel at home at home. This is a place where daily efforts must be made to jerk oneself out of boredom.

Yet, all sorts and types of people can be found here living, studying, plying their trades and professions. Traffic pours down Tower Bridge Road relentlessly on weekday afternoons. People from all over London and perhaps the whole world get down here on Friday mornings for the antiques market. Guys Hospital, London Bridge, Southwark Cathedral, the Tower of London: all landmarks just outside this place remind us that however inert we may have become, the great world is on our doorstep.

There is anxiety here too: anxiety about a place which once hummed with industry: Christy's the hatters (in Newham's Row, off Bermondsey Street closed in 1971 after 196 years of business); Martin's the fur merchants (at the Alaska Building in Grange Road), Crosse and Blackwell's pickles in Crimscott Street, Jacob's biscuits in Wolseley Street; Peek Freans in Drummond Road (in Mill Street from 1858-1892) were all here once. Long ago, a very long time ago, Bermondsey Abbey was once here; now flattened into oblivion beneath the car park, jeered at by the advertising hoardings, forgotten by the bric-à-brac dealers on Friday mornings.

If you pore over the London A-Z you will spot many street names reminding you of much that has disappeared, and of individuals long gone and forgotten. Just who were Mr Wild (Wild's Rents), Mr Griggs (Grigg's Place) Mr Crosby (Crosby Row), Mr Tyers (Tyers Gate)? for instance, you may wonder. The mind reels at the thought of all the life this place has seen, reels and then sinks into a kind of bemused numbness.

# CATASTROPHIC DISTURBANCE: Five years on, September 1997

Five years have now passed by, and I am in the same place. What happens to us all in the course of five years? Have we changed, are we still the same, where are we now, five years on? It is possible that nothing at all changes, that we remain for ever as we were when we became newly emerged young adults. Our emotional web as then still sustains us: then as now and forever, perhaps, a sense of colossal expectation, and untold dread...

Yet, new and manifold events go on all around us: a longed for new government takes office, fresher, younger faces, more vibrant voices impinge on our consciousness. Fifteen years on, after a fairy tale marriage, an event of catastrophic disturbance happened in September, 1997 after one of the hottest Augusts on record: a nation has lost its people's princess. One Saturday, in early September, hastily arranged, the public funeral was staged at Westminster Abbey. I lay on my bed in my bedsitter in front of my small black and white TV set and watched the strange and extraordinary ceremonies unfold, all happening so near, just across the river from Bermondsey: the five grief stricken men and boys, representing three generations, the slow turning of the wheels and the click of the horses' hooves, and the continual throwing of flowers before the procession; behind, not military parades, but a whole army of representatives of countless charities the princess had worked with. Then there was the outpouring of musical lamentation during the service: music from Verdi's Requiem, pieces by English composers: William Croft, and John Taverner, a reading from Corinthians by the Prime Minister, a passionate address by the eldest brother greeted with rippling applause, a song by a famous pop star, soon to rocket, we have been told, into the number one best-selling hit of all time. An hour later the long, slow journey to the ancestral home began: through London, down motorways, and on through the shires: a solitary car protected by an escort of policemen on motorbikes, and everywhere, continually, the throwing of flowers, and rippling applause; the eventual arrival at the ancestral home, the clanging of the shutting gates, guarded by two policemen, and the private burial on an island in grounds of great tranquillity.

I wandered around in the streets of Bermondsey afterwards, and for the rest of the day pondered on the significance of these scenes: the start of an age of new intimacy, said one commentator, the gradual winding down of the monarchy until we become a republic,thought another.

All this emotion, all these images of poetic symbolism were quite spontaneous: an expression of adoration of everything we in the late twentieth century hunger so much for: a capacity to love, to love greatly, and without bounds, to know vibrant life, and radiant health, to have magnetising beauty, and a place of true significance in the wide world: all this is denied to the majority by circumstances, by the way things are done, and perhaps by a stifling lack of true self worth.

But, at last, I concluded, the hearts of the many had been prised open, so late in the day, after centuries of stifling restraint, we were finally being admonished by a princess, now gone for ever, to let our souls sing. So I thought that strange Saturday afternoon.

# A DAILY DISTURBANCE OF NOISE WITHOUT END

Today, and tomorrow, and for evermore, daily existence means trying to tolerate the random jangle of contemporary inner city noise: sounds are emitted by humans, animals, machines and objects alike, as pervasive as rubbish, as pestering as the paper and packaging that surrounds almost every transaction today.

At the start of another day there is the clicking of door latches, bunches of door keys jingling as doors are locked, or jangling on the floor when inevitably dropped. I hear pigeons gurgling as they swoop down on pieces of stale bread outside the window, mad cackling laughter erupts down the corridor, chairs start creaking overhead. There was one morning when a door overhead was being slammed shut almost every ten minutes it seemed. What could all this be about? I wondered. There is always someone hammering or banging at something. There is always the dull, slurring buzz of vehicles on the streets. To be valid, contemporary noise must be repetitive, pulsating, obsessional; must strive to drive anyone listening almost crackers. Fire alarms on shops outside can detonate for up to half an hour: eventually someone may turn up, someone may contrive to switch it all off. Pop music may blare out of an open window from the estate opposite for hours on end on Saturdays. Then there are the times, any time, when the fire alarm goes off in the building I am in; not just one, but countless alarms, a colossal chorus of alarms ringing and ringing from every nook and cranny; picking up a whiff of smoke from somewhere they do their work too efficiently.

At the start of the evening there is often the insistent bouncing of a football on the pavement outside as Bermondsey youth goes out to play. From the room next door to me there is often student chatter, one voice excited, the other quiet and low. There was one night when the Indian student was giving an English pronunciation lesson to the Chinese boy. Over and over again, he made him say a monosyllabic word; was it doll, was it dog? I couldn't quite make it out.

At night time there is often tension and anguish down the road outside: police cars screeching away after their victims, ambulances fleeing down the road, conveying away the sick and dying with desperate urgency.

But as the day winds down, from about seven o'clock in the evening, the streets start to empty, people are home again for a meal and rest. As darkness descends a strange sadness seems to prevail, after the exertions of the day, after a day that many may have spent quite chaotically; sadness gives way to silence, and stillness, and finally to sleep; sleep which so often was denied me when I was living across the river in the lands of the little monsters.

Note: Noise is a major pollutant and irritant of our times. Southwark News, May 22nd 1997 carried a short article with the headlines: 'Stop that flaming row' Record number of complaints over hot weekend...New Age rave on Old Kent Road...Fisher late night party...noise officials overwhelmed with calls.'

# RETURN TO THE REALM OF BOREDOM

Five years on, still, the dark, ominous cloud of boredom hangs heavily so often. What is the origin of this state? Where does this dullness and emptiness of spirit and mind, and lethargy of body come from? On Saturdays it is there at its most pervasive, the day after the exertions and tensions of the week. Even worse is the time at Christmas when everything goes totally silent; when you go plunging down into a deep crevasse. I often ask myself one probing question: what would happen to me, how would I feel if I moved away for ever, went to a provincial town, said goodbye to the big city forever?

Every week, it seems, there is a never ending craziness, a sense of disturbance without end; piles and piles of papers and books go cascading; the second hand of the alarm clock started going backwards one day; the endless muddle-ups and delays; the failure of all efforts at communication; and the nagging sense that ahead lie only years of solitude, and just muddling through, and forever, as always, being quite clueless as to what exactly it is that I should be doing; just what it is that society desires from me (and then the obvious answer: that it desires nothing except my money to buy their products, and goods and services).

We are all the victims, perhaps of a capitalist society which is too overloaded: with too many products, too many images, too much information, too much news; and then too many people, and for far too long, too much change. But, is it possible that everything is all quite wrong, is it possible that we are all entirely wrong, in every conceivable direction?

And finally, there is this very city itself: a city without end, from which escape so often seems impossible; a city so full of edifices and institutions, banks and chambers; the very name London conveying a sense of weight and worthiness, of museums and monumentality: a city so vast that it simply swallows up people, never to be seen, or heard of again.

# AN MP's IMPRESSIONS OF BERMONDSEY

Simon Hughes is Bermondsey's Social and Liberal democrat MP. You will often see him in Bermondsey travelling around in his orange taxi on his endless business. Even on Christmas Day he is out and about, visiting the lonely and needy. Re-elected now five times back to Parliament he has an actor's chameleon like ability to blend in with all and sundry, to partake at least momentarily in the lives and concerns of all he encounters. Indeed it should be so with any people's representative who knows that his duty is to articulate the views of a whole, diverse community.

The following article 'Out of the cupboard' was first published by the evening Standard in their 'Why I live in...' series, in their issue of 29th August 1990, and it is reprinted here, courtesy of Simon Hughes. It is a telling reflection of his identification and involvement with the locality . Eight years on, he reflects on changes he has experienced in a special interview (Fifteen years of Simon Hughes, MP) in Southwark News, February 26th, 1998. He was also profiled in the same paper, February 25th 1993.

I came here for work. It was very simple really. When I started as a pupil barrister in the old days, when you got no income at all - I needed to live somewhere within cycling distance of the Temple and in the cheapest accommodation I could find.

There were three of us in the same straits. Starting a career with no money, we scoured inner London for somewhere suitable to life. We used to go out looking in an old Austin A40, a bicycle strapped on the top. We would park the car, take off the bike and the three of us would do concentric circles - one on foot, one on two wheels and one on four - looking for possible homes.

But, in the end, shelter came from another direction. An old friend from college had moved to London to run a youth organisation in North Camberwell. They wanted youth workers and offered accommodation over the shop.

So the three of us moved into a very cheap flat in a solid old vicarage, just a few yards off the Old Kent Road. I stayed there for six years while undergoing my indoctrination in how to be "streetwise" in the inner city of the 1970's. Kids on the run from the police, kids trying to beat up their parents or kids trying to beat up - and in one or two cases kill - each other were the regular fare. Real hard community politics did not take long to learn. But when I got heavily into party politics, I had to give up the youth work, so they threw me out. A friend put me up and I lived in what was all but a cupboard.

Indeed, when I was selected as a candidate for Bermondsey I was still living in the cupboard. Desparately I searched the constituency for somewhere just slightly more secure. It was very hard to find anywhere to rent, let alone buy in Bermondsey, with owner-occupation at 2.2 per cent and 80 per cent of all property owned by the council - I think there was a total of six properties for sale!

We found one which had the appealing features of a kitchen extension with sliding patio doors, a little garden and a sauna in the basement. There were a few snags: we discovered the kitchen extension had not been given planning permission; the sauna was there because it had been a "private club" with a dubious history; and a garden full of cannabis.

Negotiations broke down when the owner got locked up - but I suppose that's par for the course in a constituency where many more than the average number of people go away for unintended holidays as guests of Her Majesty.

At last I found an upstairs maisonette for sale in Lynton Road, just the other side of the Old Kent Road and almost immediately behind the Dun Cow. It is in an area that was beautified in the Twenties when one of my illustrious predecessors Dr Salter, and his progressive wife Ada, realised that one of the best ways to improve the health of the people was to improve their environment.

They planted trees in each road as well as building the first council houses (and municipal sauna) and did lots of other good things, the legacy of which is still with us in the physical layout of Bermondsey today.

I moved into the top half of the house but it wasn't long before the bottom half came up for sale (if you were living below a General Election campaign wouldn't you move?) People often say to me as I go about my business: "You don't know what it's like", when they are talking about the lack of rubbish collection, or the squatters next door. I think I do. My place is at the end of a small terrace. The rest of the terrace was falling down, then empty, then squatted, and only just now, after seven years, has been done up and occupied.

Behind me there were derelict council sheds with inglorious corrugated iron, squatted by that least quiet of neighbours, a car-body repair shop. One night I woke up thinking: isn't it noisy? Isn't it light? Isn't it warm? And then realised the building next door was ablaze and flames were licking the side of my home. Just another arson atrack.

Then they decided to demolish the haulage yard opposite. Sitting in my little garden one sunny summer's afternoon, with band rehearsal on one side, panel-beating on the other, demolition opposite and a plane flying overhead, I thought: Inner city life? This is what it's all about.

And now even my haven - my little garden - has been under attack. One morning a couple of weeks ago I was in the shower when the contractor, working for the local council which had decided to replace the corrugated iron shed by a local housing office, suddenly demolished my garden wall.

By accident of course ... even more accidental than the council decision to put a housing office next to me. "If you're not satisfied with what we are doing you know where you can go." Next door. As soon as they open, I'll be first in the queue.

But in spite of all this, and the fact that the local form of exchange and mart means I have increasingly to make the place look like Fort Knox, it is a good place to be - a real community with real live community politics to get involved with.

There are the battles to increase low-cost housing for those who want to rent or buy against the pressure to price everything out of the range of 99 per cent of locals; the battles to make sure the regeneration of Docklands is conservation and not destruction of all the community holds dear; the battle to force the Government to commit itself to give us the Bermondsey Tube station on the Jubilee Line (I will certainly throw a political fit if we don't).

It is all very well other people writing about how wonderful their area is, but ours holds not only some of the best of old London and the best of the new, it was once London's throbbing and working heart. And if you look at the map it is the centre still.

Above: *Bombed out Bermondsey,* conté crayon drawing by Ethel Gabain, 1941. Courtesy: South London Gallery. The women discuss practicalities, the boys look on aimlessly. Bermondsey's chief librarian, 1923-1950, James Stewart wrote an account *Bermondsey in War, 1939-1945* published by The Bermondsey and Rotherhithe Society in 1980.

# THE BERMONDSEY 'SPIRIT': some observations from the 1920's

The following article 'Down in Bermondsey by a resident' appeared in the Daily Express on 4th May, 1929. It is reproduced courtesy of the Daily Express:

If you enter Tower Bridge road from the Old Kent Road you will find yourself in Bermondsey.

You will smell smells from fish stalls and old clothes barrows ... from jellied eel shops that have basins of grey liquid in the windows, with fat sausages and meat pies alongside them.

You will find fish and chip saloons, with clouds of hot fishy vapour curling out of the doors, and red posters in the windows advertising the programme at the local picture palace. Great warehouses, factories, and blocks of tenements loom up all round.

In spite of this Bermondsey has a spell. The people who live within its bounds are as unsnobbish as the fisherfolk in a Donegal coast hamlet.

Bermondsey square, where I live, is the site of old Bermondsey Abbey. And they say it rivalled Westminster itself in the days before the Dissolution. Foundries, tan yards, and various public works surround Bermondsey square now.

At the very gates of the old abbey, too, there is now a building called the Great Central Hall, with swing doors and a grand organ. It is owned by the South London Mission, and in it they sing Wesleyan hymns with gusto every Sunday night.

Look down any side street off Tower Bridge road, and you are likely to see a draggled man walking slowly in the middle of the road and trying to sing.

He looks expectantly up at the windows; then you hear a copper jingling down on the road, and the old fellow ambles off, breaking his song, to pick it up.

You may see another of the sorrowful brotherhood with a barrel organ, and children gathered round lilting and dancing to the music. The man growls at them to go away, for they distract the attention of potential almsgivers from himself.

Sunday is visiting day in Bermondsey. Relatives come to tea, and a social evening with the gramaphone, or community singing, is the rule.

The music is not highbrow. The songs are nearly always "wondering" songs, and about "caring" and "remembering" and "pals" and "wonderful girls".

They sing the same ones over and over again.

Sometimes, especially when beer has formed part of the entertainment, shrill voices are raised in argument, and the noise of breaking crockery mars the conviviality, but that is nothing - in Bermondsey.

Above: *Arched entrance to Neckinger Estate*; a drawing from Bermondsey Walk leaflet, London Borough of Southwark, 1984. Courtesy: L.B.S.

# SOME TRIBUTES TO BERMONDSEY AND ROTHERHITHE FOLK

Former Bermondsey vet Iain Bownes comments (Southwark News, August 2nd, 1997):

"I like the people round here as they are like Australians. They are straight-forward and say what they think. They respect you for good service but will come down on you like a tonne of bricks if you con them...I like the traditional Bermondsey clients - the larger than life characters who always have a joke a minute. Sometimes you can't shut them up. Now people with more money have come into Bermondsey. It's not that the community spirit has been lost. I'm a Millwall fan and the club links everyone together. I felt sad for locals when they were not doing well. But when they do well you see it in the smiles on people's faces. People have had it so hard around here for so long, but they have got so much determination. I see my own situation reflected in theirs."

Father Nick Richards, has, not unnaturally, experienced more of the inner emotions of the community. 'Pie'n Liquor' is the quarterly newsletter of St. Mary's. In the Autumn 1997 issue he published an article 'A reflection after 20 years'. He observes:

"...and what of friends and 'characters'? Too many to count, but never too many to remember with gratitude and thanks. Rotherhithe has taught me so much and has confirmed what I always thought - directness and down to earthiness are far preferable to fancy words and flannel. My two abiding impressions, after 20 years, are of laughter and tears. The humour of people, and the quick wit, and the softness of people, under a seemingly hard exterior, and the unselfconscious way in which so many tears are shed. I reckon that Rotherhithe has made me a more feeling person than I ever was..."

In Southwark News, May 21st, 1992, he commented:

"... I have never been shocked by the things I have seen, but I do get upset with sad things, with the violence, and the cruelty. I'm never surprised at the ways of humanity - no parish priest should be - but I do get very disappointed by great selfishness and hatred, by people who have no comprehension of forgiveness, of trying to get on with life..."

Roman catholic priest Father John Clark (formerly at Our Lady of the Immaculate Conception, Surrey Docks) comments (Southwark News, January 26th, 1995), more briefly:

"Bermondsey people are quite remarkable. They are very courteous, but they are also quite straight and old fashioned in a way."

**The City panorama, from London Bridge to Tower Bridge:**

The view eastwards, from London Bridge includes:

Cannon Street Station, John Hawkshaw & J. W. Barry, 1866; Mondial House, Hubbard Ford & Partner, 1973; Ebgate House, Holford Associates, 1977; Fishmongers Hall, Henry Robert, 1834; Adelaide House, Sir John Burnet and Tait, 1925; Magnus House, Richard Seifert, 1977; Montague House, Covell Matthews, Wheatley, 1989; Barclays International Bank, Fenchurch St, City of London Real Property Co, 1968; National Westminster Bank, Richard Seifert, 1981; Kleinwort Benson, Fenchurch Street, City of London Real Property Co, 1963-8; Billingsgate Market, former market Sir Horace Jones, 1875, refurbished Richard Rogers, 1989; St. Dunstan in the East, Wren, (steeple, 1697-99); Lloyds of London, Richard Rogers, 1986; Minster Court, GMW Partnership, 1990; Custom House, David Lang, 1812-17, centre rebuilt Sir Robert Smirke, 1825; Vincula House, City of London Real Property Co, 1962-65; Sugar Quay, Fitzroy Robinson, 1977; Three Quays, Yates, Cook and Darbyshire, 1958; Tower of London.

# THE BRIDGE, THE BIG BRIDGE: Tower Bridge

This is the bridge you cross to get to, and also from Bermondsey: if you are a Londoner you may well cross the bridge on foot weighed down by the sheer vastness of the capital city, and of your own utter insignificance in it, overstrained with the burden of trying to make ends meet, ever aware of the infinite, incalculable wealth of the city beyond, forever beyond grasp and penetration. The Londoner wending his weary way across the bridge to the underground station may perhaps hear in his head the slow, plodding steps of the last movement of Benjamin Britten's third string quartet, one of his very late works. No-one can possibly observe all those who pass over the bridge; all those with whom society does not know what to do. Those who drift apart, become forgotten, forgotten that is, if ever known...

Or, on other days, the lonely Londoner may feel an upsurge of infinite rage and frustration: and shake a clenched fist at the buildings on the other side: UGLY, UGLY, UGLY, he may screech out. Or else, a concerned, curious visitor accompanying his host may observe somewhat diplomatically: 'You English have a curious aesthetic sense'; may well wonder to himself what is exactly wrong with this English race; so energetic, so clever, so brilliant in so many ways, yet also so crass, so blind, so insensitive.

And then there is the Tower...Standing on the bridge and scrutinising the panoramic view to the west, one thought seems to prevail: that this impregnable, ancient fortress will survive long after all the pretentious, power crazy, absurd blocks nearby have gone. Amassed around Minster Court, with the old Port of London building as advance guard, and the Monument and St Paul's Cathedral at the rear, these buildings have launched a sustained assault on the ancient fortress to no avail: squat, dumpy, of great antiquity, it speaks to us today of rock hard stubbornness, unyielding hardness and obdurate durability for centuries to come.

Yet, whatever your initial mood, no-one crossing the bridge can fail to be moved by its optimism, its sense of pride and confidence, cannot fail to notice to frequent invocations to the Almighty: the motto of the City Corporation: 'Domine dirige nos' (may God direct us). Here on this extraordinary bridge people from the entire world pass by, carrying all kinds of messages on their clothing; their bags, shirts, shorts and caps; they parade past, advertising brand names, universities, sports clubs and messages they wish to convey to the world. One hot summer day a boy stripped off his shirt to be photographed by his adoring girl friend; one evening I observed two people who were toasting some special occasion you and I could know nothing about. The orientals point their cameras and video machines at this monument as soon as they are there; Germans exclaim: 'So viel zu sehen' (so much to see). It is all a moving and curiously touching spectacle.

Above: *The early 18th century vicarage of the old St John's church,* Tower Bridge Road. The tall chimney stacks are reflected in the 1970's mission building.

Opposite: A drawing by Ernest Hasseldine, form *The Glory in the garret,* Epworth Press, 1932. The money lender to the right highlights the poverty of an area so close to the City.

Above: *Linocut by Stephen Mumberson:* part of his series of London landmarks and monuments, 1991-4; a loving, jewel-like depiction of many a Londoner's favourite landmark. Glyn Thomas' recent etching *Tower Bridge* (shown at the Royal Society of Painter-Engravers 1997 show) expresses a comparable affection, but shows a vista extending from the Houses of Parliament to Canary Wharf.

Above: *Tower Bridge as a backcloth for a nonsensical drama;* this ink drawing by John Vernon Lord comes from his brilliant collection *The Nonsense Verse of Edward Lear,* Jonathan Cape, 1984, and illustrates the 'old Person of Ems, who casually fell in the Thames...' John Brunsden has made a coloured print of a very similar view, but it is a day time scene with swirling orange clouds.

# TOWER BRIDGE ROAD TRISECTED

This main thoroughfare road falls quite neatly into three sections: the part to and from Tower Bridge: the shops and businesses on the eastern side vying for visitor and tourist trade, *Tower Bridge Court*, 1990, architects: Cecil, Denny, Highton, at one end, and the former *Tower Bridge Hotel*, of almost one hundred years earlier, at the Tooley Street end. Then there is the stretch dominated by large buildings: *Tower Bridge School*, the *London City Mission* to the north of the blue bridge, the *Cat and Cucumber cafe* on the corner of Druid Street, then the *old vinegar works Sarsons*, and the old 1909 *National Leathersellers College* opposite. Antique businesses then follow on in old warehouses and factory buildings. Beyond the Grange Road junction the third section, again different: with its jumble of ever changing shops it turns into a typical London high street. Here is a street (originally Bermondsey New Road) which suggests the atmosphere of the early 1970's: a street reminding me often of my earliest years in the capital city.

I recall the time when I sat in a Wimpey bar in North London, scribbling down ideas onto a brown paper bag for countless publishing projects. What has become of all those brainwave ideas today? Today, some years, really many years later, I find myself sitting again alone in the newly opened *Tower Kebab Restaurant*, asking myself repeatedly why today everything seems to have fallen apart, whether or not everything has in fact gone quite hopelessly wrong. These dark moments, no doubt afflict many a city dweller; but it often seems that society today has fallen into a state of perplexity and bafflement. No-one seems to understand anything at all any longer. What should be the goals of an individual's existence? What is life actually for; to whom should we turn for help with these conundrums? But I must get on with this chapter, it is time to get out and about, looking and recording.

*The Pagoda pub*, at the Webb Street corner alongside *Brighton Buildings*, 1892, brings zest to the street at its centre. In the late 1980's trendy new businesses opened in the ground floor shops of Brighton Buildings: *Yum Yum* (children's' wear), *Pretty Steps* (exclusive Italian and Spanish shoes), *Curiosity* (cards and gifts), for instance. Today they have all gone, replaced by others: *Unique touch* (hair and beauty salon), the *Party Specialist Shop*, the *Rock Christian Bookshop*, *Revival* (hairdressers), Afro-Caribbean foods. There is competition across the road: *Harmony*, hair salon and cosmetics is at number 53; at number 71 another party shop: the *Sweetie Palace* whose products include personalised cakes.

Most of the shops in this high street have flats above or behind them, but a chartered surveyor *Cyril Silver and Partners* have their offices above the launderette at number 44. A new Chinese medicine shop has recently opened at number 96, and next door there is an African barbers called *Clipmasters*. At 86a is *Roxlee's the City Cobblers* run by Patrick Cleary and Danny Rutherford, here for some 18 years (featured in South London Press, January 16th, 1998). Across the road at number 87 is *M. Manze*, famous for its eels, pies and mash and attracting much custom from over the bridge. The business is run today by three brothers, Graham, Geoff and Rick Poole, grandsons of Michele Manze (son in law of original proprietor in the late nineteenth century Robert Cooke). A new shop is to open in Sutton and an article on this occasion was published in Southwark News, February 12th, 1998. There is also a Manze shop at 105 Peckham High Street.

*Haddon Hall Baptist Church* at number 22 is a modern day continuation of the mission hall situated on the other side of the road, and commemorating the evangelist Charles Haddon Spurgeon. The church has just started up a stylish newsletter and issue number two, Autumn 1997 reports on the summer time Chatterbox Club for 5-11 year olds, attracting some 86 children and bringing in students from Colorado Springs and different parts of Britain; Simon Crisp the minister is shown with his head in the stocks, and enjoying an ice lolly in another photograph. Further down Leroy Street, behind the Baptist church you find a *Celestial Church of Christ* in premises formerly occupied by a shoe wholesaler.

Opposite the Baptist church is the *George pub*. Across the road we are jerked into the present day: the *Favorite Chicken and Ribs take-away*, an off-licence *Tower Wine*, and at numbers 35-37 *Twin Wheelers, motorcycles*; then comes the *Shakti Authentic Indian cuisine*, a shop *Tola Reuben Ltd*, selling 'general goods and business services'.

Progressing further down the road, a new nursing home, opened 1998, has been built on a previously vacant site on the eastern corner; beyond lies the flyover, and underground subways; a bleak conclusion to the road at the Old Kent and New Kent roads junction.

Above: *Turret of the disused Tower Bridge Hotel*, corner of Tooley St, Tower Bridge Road; built 1897, Architect: W.A.Withall. Photograph of building in its original glory as hotel and bar in SBR, II. Currently being converted into a Wetherspoon pub.

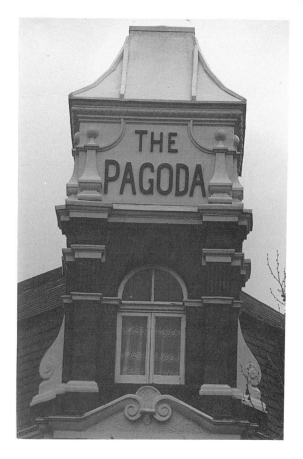

Above: *Turret of the Pagoda pub*, Tower Bridge Road (on corner of Webb Street).

Above: *The old Tabard Centre*, part of Southwark's Adult Education; previously a London School Board building, erected 1873; now (as from 1996) a converted block of 16 private flats. Faces new block of St Olave's Girls School, New Kent Rd.

Opposite: a drawing by Ernest Hasseldine, from *The Glory in the garret*, Epworth Press, 1932 (account of South London Mission). The market no longer extends to the mission and does not operate on Sunday's.

It is of all the street markets in London, that which to onlookers strikes most deeply the note of poverty.

Mr Charles Booth "Religious Life of London"

SUNDAY MORNING STREET MARKET TOWER BRIDGE ROAD

The most dramatic change to the landscape down here must surely be the private residential block *Trocette Mansion* (initially named Tower Bridge Mansions). The Trocette cinema stood on the site since the 1930's before becoming vacant land. The archaeologists came first to unearth the foundations of the old abbey (see article in Southwark News, August 17th, 1995). I watched cement being poured into the foundations of the new block; slowly the walls went up; the contractors did their jobs and then departed for the next. Could one say, perhaps, that this Bellway Homes development seems at present like a bizarre intrusion into the old London atmosphere already alluded to above? Comparing and contrasting this building's style and design with that of the South London Mission opposite, and almost a century apart, one might observe that something has gone horribly wrong in society. Look at the mean, little fake balconies, suggesting a gagged and silenced community within. Look at the two turrets with their lid like, containing and frustrating uppermost structures, and the spear-headed railings with tiny urns. The pigeons, for sure, have not found a home here; they remain squatting on the cornices of the old shops and flats across the road (with their intriguingly varied attic windows).

Moving up Tower Bridge Road this old and contemporary London atmosphere quickly disperses as we pass into Antiques Land, a continuation eastwards of the antiques trading at the lower end of Bermondsey Street. Oh yes, Bermondsey, the place for antiques, many will tell you. Yet, is it possible that as the next century progresses all this will vanish, move away to other parts? There are plans my informant tells me for the redevelopment of the site adjacent to the churchyard, a new hotel may be built next to Tower Gate, site of the old, S.Rowe leather factory (see article in Southwark News February 12th, 1998); number 168, the Antiques Exchange (currently occupied by Cannonbury Antiques) has been sold. The *Compactum* antiques warehouse in Newhams Row (bottom of Bermondsey Street), is now being converted. Lorries of scaffolding were there when I was around one December morning. I heard a property man with a file of papers declare quite emphatically 'Very well'.

Currently the antiques trading scene in Tower Bridge Road is as follows:
*Richard Tindall* (antiques reproductions) is at number 151. I have wandered round their showroom there on several occasions, have observed the bird cages, the teddy bear pictures, the boxing booth panels; at number 155 there is another yard with various businesses and it leads into the rear of Newhams Row. The *Old Cinema Antiques Warehouse* is at number 157, here for some five years. It is the Bermondsey branch of the Old Cinema Antiques Department Store (in a former cinema) at 160, Chiswick High Street, which has been trading for 17 years. The proprietor is Martin Hanness. The Bermondsey warehouse is a colossal place, model aeroplanes hang from the ceilings and all floors are crammed full. The firm has a special interest in the decorative arts 1880-1940, especially at their Chiswick shop and this speciality is highlighted in their newsletter 'Antique Post' issue number five. A London riverside mural by South London artist Philipe Delestre decorates the entrance, where anything might be displayed, catching one's attention on the way to the bridge. *Tower Bridge Antiques* is at 159-161; run by Cyril Kaye there are endless rooms full of furniture. *Tower Gate* next door houses offices of Customs and Excise. On the corner of Tanner Street is the London Glass Services business (in former pub). Across the road you find the *Antiques Exchange,* run by Robert Draysey. Several years ago he found a model of Tower Bridge in an Essex back garden, and a photograph of this and him on it appeared in the Evening Standard, February 22nd, 1993. Indeed, he has a knack for tracking down the unusual. His shop is quite unlike any others in Bermondsey: an Aladdin's cave crammed full of curious and beautiful objets d'art. *Oola Boola Antiques* at 166 is run by Robert Scales and has been here since 1979. They occupy a building formerly owned by W.H.Hobbs & Co who handled oils and spices here until the early 1970's. The names of the business comes apparently from an art deco children's story book. Outside you find signs advertising the firm's wholesale services in German, French, Spanish, Italian and Japanese. Next door you find *Europa House Antiques,* run by a Spaniard Antonio Mendoza, here since 1994, but for many years in Bermondsey Street. I looked with interest at his carefully chosen, mixed stock, and he told me of the strange ways of his British clientele.

Beyond antiques land lie the restaurants and estate agents on the eastern side of Tower Bridge. The estate agents *Duncan Allen, Alex Neil,* and *Chesterton's* all display these interior photographs we are now so accustomed to associating with new docklands properties. The Copper pub has recently changed hands and is now the *River Bar,* designed by Sampson & Associates in Mill Street. Contemporary photographs adorn the walls. Then there are the *Bridge Tandoori, Ye Old Bridge House,* and the *Trattoria sul Ponte. Tower Approach* sells an intriguing mixture of gift items. From these shops onwards the sense of a dramatic increase in tension becomes discernible: the road steepens, the great world in all its chaos impinges on our consciousness: the big city looms into our vision.

Above: *St John's, Horselydown;* drawn by G. Shepherd, engraved by W. Wise for the Architectural Series of London churches; built 1727-32, architects: Hawksmoor and John James. Bombed, its foundations were used for a new building, Nasmith House, (London City Mission), built 1972-6, architects: John D. Ainsworth & Associates. This street, home and work place evangelising organisation was founded in London by a Scotsman David Nasmith in 1835. A drawing of the bombed/derelict church is included in Geoffrey Fletcher's collection of drawings *Pearly Kingdom,* 1965.

Another eighteenth century engraving (drawn by C. Burton) was published in the first edition of this publication.

Above: *Sarson's Vinegar factory, the Tower Bridge Road courtyard;* water colour drawing,
1979, by Cyril Cooke. Courtesy: South London Gallery.

# INTO THE OLD JAM FACTORY: Hartley Business Centre

This large, rambling old place, dominated by the giant HARTLEY chimney is now being rented out to businesses and creative people by paper merchants Worsleys. Paper firms have their storage here; carpenters, designers, painters, potters all have studios and workshops in the rabbit warren of corridors in the three blocks. *Archival Record Management*, a new, but rapidly growing firm run by Sidney Hyams offers storage and retrieval services to city firms, as well as TV and film companies from one floor in A Block; *Jonathan McCree*, an art history graduate from Sussex University has had his studio next door for some seven years. His thickly painted, hermetic canvases relate to myth and private dilemma.

I was able to penetrate this colossal fortress of a place one Saturday in October when a number of artists were showing their work as part of the Southwark Festival open studios weekend. I was greeted by one artist I was especially keen to search out: the young *Emily Toscano-Heighton*; drawing inspiration from the Southwark environment, her paintings disarm one with their bright yellows and oranges and blues, and liberated small figures. Peckam has been a favourite haunt for the artist: she was displaying her painting 'Bananas under a Peckham sky' here, and later next week I saw her 'A Peckham morning' at the show in the atrium of Price Waterhouse, Number 1, London Bridge. Another painting, depicting a bawling child and mother showed an empty street with part of the Hartley block as background. Mozart's 40th symphony was playing from the artist's studio and she told me that very soon she was off to Marseilles for the next six months.

I sat down on one of *James Kibble's* comfortable 'lovers' chairs, handled the exotic pieces by ceramic artist *Sonya Kahlon* on the window ledge, stared in at a cabinet of ceramic work by *Ram Welti* who works from a studio in the corridor bridge between two blocks. I wandered away, climbed the stairs, not knowing what I would find, strayed down one corridor and found the *Palindrome Press*, a printing workshop and studio of *Tim Long* and *Clare Ruddock-West*. I urged Mr Long to show me his work, and out of his cabinet of drawers came huge prints inspired by biological imagery, a pre-occupation also shared by his partner. Somehow, both had missed out on the festival and open studio event, but I thought their work was stimulating enough for such an occasion. I wandered on up another storey to the roof top.

I gasped; here it all was; spread out on the ground below; my place; the extraordinary chaotic jumble of the inner city, the densely built up environment where countless lives are lived out. Yet once again, I was assailed by a sense of breath-taking possibility; again, a curious, yet abiding sense that I was in a territory where any one day I might be on the trail of astounding creative genius...

Above: *Hartley, the old jam factory* is a huge, rambling factory block, built in 1901. It has impressive entrance gates at the bottom of Green Walk, and is dominated by a large chimney as shown in David Fried's drawing. His cloth-capped figure stares uneasily within himself; does he recall more prosperous times? The building is now known as the Hartley Business Centre. Sherwoods is currently being redeveloped for a gospel church, with upper storeys added (Southwark News November 7th, 1996).

# BERMONDSEY STREET MUDDLE

Bermondsey Street of today is a very muddled place: many kinds of businesses and organisations and people can be found here today. At the Tooley street end you pass the former printing works of *Howard Jones*, (now being converted by Bellway Homes) at numbers 7-25, and here for some 125 years; then comes the long tunnel, and you emerge into the daylight glimpsing the tower of St. Mary Magdalene in the distance, with the sense that you are now in another distinct and separate locality. The street is one of London's most historic: it linked the abbey with river, and goes past Abbey Street and Bermondsey Square at its southern most end and concludes with the Hand and Marigold pub and the South London Mission.

This is a street which seems to be puzzled about its own identity, so confused has it become today. People rush away after business hours; by half past six in the evening the street has emptied; it sinks into silence and broods uneasily on all that it has seen.

Here is a kind of descriptive, classified directory outlining what you can find here today as at November, 1997

To start with God: an organisation called the *World Miracle Outreach* has recently moved into number 88, on the corner of Tyers Gate; and then of course, the architectural climax of the street, and its biggest surprise for any first time visitor must be the delightful gothic eccentricity of St. Mary Magdalene's street facade. The South London Mission further on is a Methodist church establishment, and much less ancient.

Then must come the *Post Office*, an important nerve centre for the entire district. Here on any day, you might encounter all kinds of people living or working, or both in the locality, or just passing through; some just chuck their day's work into the post bags and charge out hurriedly, others have time to spend with sub-postmaster Kamal Patel who serves everyone with gracious efficiency. Born in Baroda, India, he has a degree in Commerce and previously spent ten years with the Eagle Star Insurance Company.

Then we all need food and drink; you can buy your sandwiches nearby at *Goode Foods*, have a drink with your mates at the *Woolpack*, or the *Honnest Cabbage* (previously the Yorkshire Grey) also in the vicinity; then there are two traditional cafes: *Al's Cafe* at number 128, and the *Rose Cafe and Dining Room* at number 210. Inhabiting a somewhat different ambience, and attracting a clientele from much further afield there is the *Delfina* at number 50, a recent arrival.

At numbers 59-63 (old police station building), you find the headquarters of *Davy & Co Ltd.* wholesale wine merchants and operators of public houses, off-licences and wine bars. This old family firm (current chairman: James Davy) was founded in 1870 by Francis Edwin Davy. Their first house was the Rising Sun in the Strand (demolished in 1902). In 1965 they opened the Boot and Flogger in Borough High Street, moving later to 10/20 Redcross Way, and this led to considerable expansion in the field.

At number 139: *Rankin Brothers*, another old family firm established some 200 years ago on the west coast of Scotland; they specialise in cork and plastic stoppers and capsules. They are owners of 6,000 acres of cork forest in Carpucoes, Portugal. They occupied a warehouse in Abbey Street, opposite Bermondsey Square in the 1930's, and after bombing moved to their present location. Part of their premises here were sold in the 1990's for residential development (Cork House).

At numbers 176-8 you find the non-stop day and night *Ticino Bakery*, here for 20 years.

If boredom and anxiety are essential ingredients of life today, then entertainment and the arts are at hand for stimulation and escape. Art shows can be seen at the Delfina, and the Old Tannery opposite. Number 47 is an important port of call for the theatrical world: the offices of the *Stage* newspaper are here as well as the *Association of British Theatre Technicians*. Percussionists are served by Paul Hagen's establishment at number 120 (previously in Wapping); *Impact Percussion* is a retail, hire and workshop business; *American Percussion* is the wholesale distribution company.

Health and fitness are likewise obsessional preoccupations of our time. At Globe House (1903), on the corner of Crucifix Lane you find Angelika Grohmann's *Yoga Space* organisation and in Gemini House at number 180-182, the newly arrived herbal specialists the *London Clinic of Phytotherapy* (a training clinic for the School of Phytotherapy).

Then there are more mundane establishments: *The Refugee Legal Centre* operates from Sussex House at number 39-45; *SITRA* (Specialist Information Training Agency for Single Person Housing) from Bramah House at number 65-71. *Thames Reach* also here is a housing association. Business and management services are run from *Kwelm House* on the corner of Snowsfields.

Above: *Bermondsey Street, 1850's*; a drawing by H. Laverock Phillips. Courtesy: Southwark Local Studies Library. Russell Street (named after a local philanthropist who died in 1784) is now Tanner Street.

Above: *Bermondsey Street's oldest building, today's No 78,* dating from late seventeenth century, currently owned by Ash and Ash. The old Plough Inn is to the left.

Above: *Drawing of old houses (occupied by wool staplers) in Bermondsey Street,* by John Crowther; from Lost London: being a description of landmarks which have since disappeared, pictured by J. Crowther, c. 1879-87, also described by E. Beresford Chancellor.

Above: *139 Bermondsey St,* premises of Rankin Bros. & Son (corkwood growers and importers).

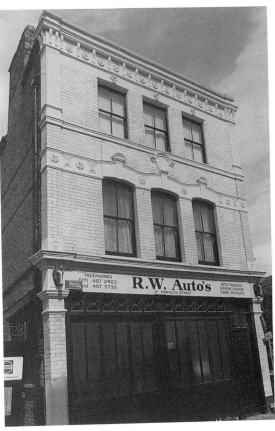

Above: *Old smithy building at top of Morocco Street* (The 'John Coleman forge'); the unusually decorative upper floors are in private residential ownership.

Scientists and engineers also come to work in Bermondsey Street: *Dr. Bernard Dyer and Partners,* and *E.R. Bolton* are chemical analysts, and operate from number 73-77. Dr. Dyer set up his agricultural chemistry laboratory in 1879. *Engineering Design Consultants* at number 106 moved to the old Midland Bank on the corner of Morocco Street in 1991, from Bloomsbury. Established in 1969, they offer a full range of specialist building trade services.

The *General Ironfoundry Co* are builders' merchants, established in 1852 and they operate today from premises in Royal Oak Yard. *MTM (Maintenance and Technical Management)* is at number 194; *How Engineering Services* were also here until recently in the adjacent block. *ADT Security Systems* is at Titan House, numbers 184-192.

Antiques can bring comfort and luxury to all who earn a living in the hard world, and there is a range of businesses at the lower end of the street: *Cecilia Foley* is at number 42, on the corner of Lamb Walk; *Bermondsey Antique Traders* is at 168, *Euro Antiques* to the left of Royal Oak Yard; *Georg Wissinger* is at number 166, and *G. Viventi* at the towering number 173; in the *Antiques Pavilion* in Newhams Row businesses currently include: *Enfield Antiques* (Mr. Cassido), and *Mr Pickwick* (John Sturton). *Penny Farthing Antiques* is at number 177 and *Richard Tindall* (wholesale antique reproductions and manufacturers) have their showroom at number 212. Here you find a shop crammed full of ornamental candle sticks, walking sticks, decorative water cans, large pots, china shoes, lamp shades and dancing girls.

This is also a street for printers, designers, architects and crafts people. *Robin Greenwood* specialises in the design of architectural metal work at number 175 (Block K). *Eiler & Cox* at number 130 are chartered designers. *Dransfield Design*, architects operate from one floor of an attractive new warehouse style block they designed themselves, at the top of Morocco Street. Celebrated fashion designer *Zandra Rhodes* runs her company from numbers 79-85 (the old Arpino Gibbs building), and her museum of fashion and textiles is planned to open here soon. Almost all of Bermondsey's former leather trade firms have now gone, but there is a survivor in Bermondsey Street: *A.E. Bickel* at numbers 151-155, was established in 1938 and sold to present day managing director G.E.Job in the late 1940's. They specialise in manufacturing industrial leather and canvas goods - cash bags, cases for computers, and so on. Bookbinders *Sangorski and Sutcliffe* were founded in 1901, Zaehnsdorf in 1842; in 1988 they amalgamated and are now based at number 175 (Block R). Some two dozen staff work on the fullest range of commissions. In today's machine obsessed, machine saturated world, the survival of an enterprise so dependent on manual dexterity for all its processes is a triumph indeed.

So much then for the thrusting and clamorous activity of the business community. At weekends, and every evening, all goes quiet and then there is an opportunity to study and survey the architecture of the street more closely, impressive at its upper and lower ends, much less so in the centre. We are in a conservation area, specially chosen for a big injection of restoration money from the government and council and much work is currently in progress. Numbers 74-78 (currently owned by *Ash and Ash*) and the adjacent numbers 68-72, a mid eighteenth century former coaching inn preserve the old world atmosphere of the street, as evoked in H. Laverock Phillips' drawing. Number 78 is late seventeenth century, distinguished by its oriel window and weather boarding on its uppermost floor. The old Tempo leather factory, at number 55 is currently undergoing restoration; architect: George Legg, it dates from 1873 and was built for Oastler Palmer & Co. *Bramah House* (green, orange, cream) at numbers 65-71 is an example of contemporary warehouse restoration; and across the road the renovated warehouses in Tyers Gate currently await the first new occupants. The former police station at number 59, and the former pub next door at number 63 with stuccoed decorative upper floor panels are equally noteworthy. Today the street has only two pubs: the *Woolpack*, dating from 1720, and the younger *Yorkshire Grey* (now the Honnest Cabbage), both conveying the spirit of a bygone age. The new lettering on the Woolpack is distinctive, and the old Yorkshire Grey distinguished by its variety of window sizes, its three gables and two chimney stacks.

We sense this bygone, more civilised age, again at the lower end of the street. The old Time and Talents building, at 187 and 189, now in private ownership dates from 1907, the former rectory (now converted into five apartments), set back from the street at 191 from about 1830, and the remodelled facade of St. Mary Magdalene from the same time. *Gemini House* at numbers 180-182 across the road can also give pleasure: a decorative facade, with wrought iron ground floor grilles, blue painted window colonnettes on three floors, patterned brickwork and a new top floor extension. Most of this building is in private residential ownership.

I walked out one cold November night to check the accuracy of my observations. A ceremony for the 1997 Financial Times architectural awards was taking place at the *Delfina*. Workers were leaving the *Ticino Bakery*. People, all alone, were walking home late from work. It was impossible to know of what they were thinking. A boy slammed his front door shut and charged down the street towards the lit up tunnel. But, otherwise the street that night was very quiet. After the day's efforts it seems as if the whole place had sunk into inertia and obscurity. It was quite impossible to know what was going on in lit up rooms behind drawn curtains.

Yet again I found myself drawn away from facts and observations, and felt only the intense sadness and loneliness of it all. Again, a stabbing moment of self-interrogation: what had I been doing with myself for all my years in London? How was I going to get through all the years ahead?

Opposite: *Gemini House, 180-182,* Bermondsey Street. Formerly office accommodation the building was converted by Callington Estates into seven loft apartments, a herbal clinic, and refurbished accommodation for a fashion design company.

Above: *The early nineteenth century watch house* on corner of Abbey Street and Bermondsey Street. At one time in the 1920's it was in use as a laundry office. It was restored in 1997 (by Camberwell firm HCS Building Contractors) and may be used as a tourist/information kiosk.

At the same time, an imitation, trompe l'oeil watch-house was created on the wall of the garage of the new rectory, with a cat painted into the window (created by Bristol firm Dorothea Restoration).

# ART WORLD IN BERMONDSEY STREET

"An art gallery has opened in Bermondsey Street, up the road", I told my fish and chip man one evening, several years ago. He stared at me with incredulity.

In fact, the *Delfina Studio Trust* at number 50, the former Gardner's chocolate factory is an interesting mixture of an international artists in residence programme, a studio complex, an exhibition space, education workshops, an administrative base for the celebrated Brodsky String Quartet, and a restaurant/cafe. There is a total of 35 studios here and nine are set aside for visiting international artists; the restaurant feeds them and they are provided with accommodation in a purpose built house adjacent to the studio block. In the background, making all this possible, are art loving property consultant Digby Squires, and his wife Delfina Entrecanales (see article in Southwark News, November 3rd, 1994). The restaurant is run by caterer Stephen Congdon, with his office at number 52. He has been operating a flourishing business nationally for some 8 years, and this is his first restaurant. High profile parties and promotions are also staged here. The current publicity leaflet reads almost like a gastronomic poem; listen to the deserts on offer: mango tart tatin, sables with strawberry ice cream and raspberries, baked figs with honey and port, summer fruit trifle with syllabub, bittersweet chocolate tart with home-made vanilla ice cream, zabaglione ice cream with amaretti biscuits.

The art shows I have attended (there are some 6 a year) have not always been quite so appetising. I spoke to curator David Gillmour of my sense of the disturbance factor often discernible. I found myself worried by the horrifying mask like faces, and the death stricken sculptures by Pia Stadtbäumer (in October and November 1997); then there was a show which I would simply prefer to forget about. A sense of nightmarish horror and tragedy hardly seemed right for the enjoyment of food, I thought. And yet, as we eat, are we not often assailed by acute anxiety and indefinable dread. Is not the whole of our society now haunted by unfathomable disturbance, which commentators and academics will no doubt analyse for us all next century? But there is no doubt that fascinating art can emerge from this state of affairs, given sensitivity and artistic skill and imagination.

When the *Delfina* first opened several years ago, I was much intrigued by the prints of a Lithuanian artist Gediminas Leonavicius. Hanging on the wall above the artists' table, I found 'Waiting for the miracle': an apocalyptic meal was depicted, a vast array of figures in advanced states of drunkenness, gluttony and besotted sleep under the long table. Here was an artist with compelling vision, I thought, an artist to meet and talk with. I did not hesitate; this was one for my private little collection: a piece of art which seemed to be saying: you have got to buy this, Peter.

Across the road at the *Tannery*, I found more art of the apocalyptic tendency in prints by the young Simon Brigginshaw in a Winchester School of Art show in August 1997. All kinds of objects filled his 'wunderkammer' etchings in dream-like chaos. In a letter to me he wrote of his research in illustrated books of many kinds, of his attempt 'to convey a sense of history collapsing into entropy'. Art colleges have had shows at the Tannery in the summer months since 1996. More specialist shows have also been staged since 1994, often with intriguing titles: 'Something wrong'; 'Destroy all monsters'; 'Infinity';' 'Codes of conduct'; 'Skinning the shadow' (the body and its transient states), 'Deep end'; 'Obsession' (the nature of male preoccupations). A report I obtained from Chrisopher Pauling, the administrator, indicates that these shows attract well over 500 people. The Tannery complex is owned by Russell Gray (Shiva Ltd); there are some 16 artists' studios, and when renovated the building (the old Tempo leather factory) will probably provide office space for designers and architects. The firm also owns the old charity school building in Grange Walk.

Returning home, I frequently look sadly at a piece of public art, somewhat removed from the world of private obsession: the *Bermondsey Street mural* executed in 1981 by Lynette Lombard and her husband Vincent Milne on the wall of number 4, Tanner Street (former premises of printers John Adams). When new, it brought vibrant colour and a historical perspective to the area. Today, it has badly deteriorated, and with the building due to be redeveloped into flats and ground floor offices, there do not appear to be any plans to restore it.

March 1998: Sadly it has now all gone, sandblasted off in the last week in March and reduced to a pile of rubble.

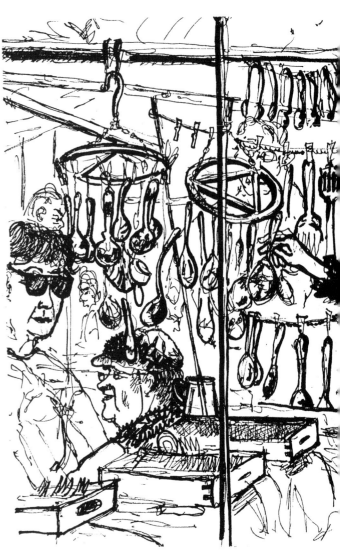

*Bermondsey Antiques Market, Bermondsey Square:* three drawings (specially commissioned) by Louise Soloway, 1992. Known historically as the New Caledonian Market, trade was conducted originally in Islington (close to the Caledonian Road) until the Second World War. Market profiled in Southwark News, February 13th, 1992 and November 23rd, 1995.

# BERMONDSEY SQUARE: Today and perhaps Tomorrow.

A poor little truncated square today: only two small wings with an antiques business on the corner, and a tiny oval of grass with roses hemmed in by privet bushes and locked gate: brushed aside, insulted almost by the expanse of car park space.

At number four, Mike and Edna Hogan provide accommodation for visiting artists and antique dealers. On several occasions I have sipped wine in the Irishman's hidden, inner courtyard and listened to his frank opinion of himself and others. Trained in hotel management in Europe he has run hotels for many years in London, experience put to good use in his own, distinctive, yet homely interior decors. 'I've had a strange life', he commented.

On Thursdays the metal stands of the market appear, and every Friday morning Bermondsey Square is transformed into the *New Caledonian Antiques Market*. From time to time I wander around the tables and stalls, looking curiously at all the stuff piled up, yet hardly ever finding anything I actually wanted to purchase; have stared at a table full of thimbles, have leafed through piles of postcards, found a pile of manuscript music once, stared with dismay at a pile of cricket bats and walking sticks scattered on the pavement; and then one Friday I came across Dickens' 'Sketches by Boz', priced £20, with fascinating illustrations by Frederick Barnard. 'Get some money', the stall holder hectored me. I knew I should not prevaricate, so I got the money and took the beautifully bound green book home with me, and plunged at once into Dickens' early descriptive pieces of London life, felt stimulated by his minute, careful observation of the human comedy, by these colourful, tableaux like evocations.

Then, on another Friday, more recently (late October 1997), I was again jerked out of mundaneness with the arrival of two cabins containing drawings and models for architects' ideas for the redevelopment of the square: new blocks to line Bermondsey and Abbey Streets, canopied areas, recreation of the Victorian square, provision for sports and events, archaeology and art features: creative, ideas schemes from Robert Ian Barnes; Renton, Howard, Wood, Levin; Ferguson McIlveen; Andrew Cowan and others, (featured in a double page article in South London Press, October 31st, 1997).

Poor, little truncated square, perhaps for not much longer then; indeed next century we may well see a startling transformation of this patch, who knows?

In the *Hand and Marigold pub* on the corner of Cluny Place, I spotted a witch on a broomstick hanging from the ceiling; magic is afoot I guessed: the Millennium is calling. I went home and played through the first movement of Beethoven's Waldstein piano sonata: the celebrated opening drumming, pommelling chords, and all the obsessional repetition that followed on seemed to be urging the whole world on and forwards, to be telling us that man is a maker, and a builder, a creature of energy and dynamism. Architects, writers, musicians, painters are all surely in the world to do just this: to drive us on, to dream dreams and visions, and keep us all for ever moving on.

Above: Two engravings of *Long Walk, opposite Bermondsey Square*, from the Builder, August 7th, 1858.

Ground plan of Bermondsey Abbey from a drawing taken in 1679.

Present plan of the Neighbourhood.

BERMONDSEY SQUARE in 1866, formerly called the COURT YARD, and originally the principal quadrangle of Bermondsey Abbey. Upon looking forward the Old Church is seen in the distance, whilst about midway on the spot now occupied by the Five Bells Public House, stood the Chapel erected in 1699 of Mr Mauduit, one of the Puritan Divines, this Chapel was afterwards a Woolwarehouse, and finally pulled down. At the opening to the Square, between the Kings John's Head Public House and the Oilshop, stood the North or great Gatehouse of the Abbey, demolished about 1807, at the back of the houses on the left, in a Builders Yard, Remains of Old Walls are to be seen. On the far corner to the right is seen the entrance to the Long Walk, here in excavating for a sewer a few years since, was discovered a stone coffin, still to be seen in the vaults of the Parish Church. Midway between the entrance to the Long Walk, and the Salt Warehouse, stood the Mansion House, which old Stowe tells us was a goodly house builded of wood and stone, the materials for which being taken from the Abbey. Turning round by the Salt warehouse, we reach the Grange Walk, here even at the present time is to be seen the East Gate House, together with the hinges upon which the gates hung, this with a few Old Houses in Bear Yard are the only remains now to be seen of this once famous Abbey.

Above:  *Bermondsey House*; watercolour drawing 1853 by T.H. Shepherd. Courtesy: Trustees of the British Museum. Built in 1541 for Sir Thomas Pope, from remains of the abbey, on site near Bermondsey Square. E.T. Clarke has some 50 pages on the building and its occupants in his history.

ST. MARY MAGDALEN, BERMONDSEY STREET, SE1.
© 1992

Above: *St Mary's Churchyard*; a view from Tower Bridge Road, drawn by Martin Millard. Highlights the fine plane tree in the centre, and the cherry trees on either side. The Lombardy Poplar, the ginko trees and the yucca plants also contribute to the special atmosphere of the churchyard. There is an account of the church written by Mervyn Wilson, 1976, with drawings and photographs.

Above: *187-189, Bermondsey Street*, the old Times & Talents building. Now converted to private flats. The settlement was here from 1889 to 1961.

Above: *Memorial fountain, in St Mary's churchyard*, to James Buckingham Bevington (1804-1892), designed by R.J. Angel (see article in London Argus, April 4, 1902).

# ST MARY'S CHURCHYARD ENCOUNTERS

In 1992, I noted:

This is a most curious churchyard: romantic, yet tame; mysterious, yet prosaic; many of the tomb stones have vanished from view: shrouded in wild ivy growths they have vanished completely; weather has eroded many of the inscriptions elsewhere: people buried here have slipped away now into oblivion; nobody remembers these people any more. This is a very ancient burial plot. At night time the trees rustle secretly: only they know of everything that has gone on on this plot of earth... But this is no film script churchyard preserved for Dickens adaptations: down and outs sit out their days here, couples sprawl on the lawns in the sun, wedding groups are photographed here, engineers, designers, doctors, antique dealers all pass through here; a violin student studies his scores; people come into this churchyard to ponder on everything, or on nothing at all; one by one they get up and depart; the pigeons swoop down on crumbs...

Then, one hot Sunday afternoon when I was sitting there alone, the decorator from Battersea appeared, asked me what I was doing there with my music, sat down and told me he knew all about Bermondsey. "A very strange park this," he said, "strange, strange people come here; this isn't a nice place, you be careful," he warned; "I've seen people robbed and beaten up here; in broad daylight too, and nobody raises a finger; two yobos nicked an old lady's handbag here, I saw it happen, chased them up Tower Bridge Road. This place is full of thieves," he warned, "all they want is your money; or else they're on skag, do you know what that is?" Who was the decorator from Battersea? Why had he walked all the way here? "I lived here for 15 years," he said. "You meet all types of people here. See the council flats over there? They're full of unemployed people, people who have got nothing." "What do they do all day long?" I asked. "They sleep, get up, talk to their neighboûrs, go to the pub, read a newspaper, eat, sleep... and then the same the next day, and the next; their kids will be like that too." "And what do they think of the business people around here? Are they jealous?" I asked. "No, they're not jealous, they look up to them, see, they respect them because they go off to work, wear smart suits, run businesses. Then, there are people with money, people who live in posh places - in Bermondsey Street, in Grange Walk." "I'm tired, I'm tired," said the decorator from Battersea; "I've got blisters on my feet, I've been walking miles. I could tell you stories, I know so many stories..."

Five years on, the churchyard remains a place of rest, of mystery, and of worrying encounters. Renovation work has progressed in recent months: paths relaid, monuments restored, railings repainted. Yet, still it is the cherry blossom in early April which catches one's attention and breath: a miraculous annual flowering, and a prelude to the hopefulness and promise of the summer months ahead. The centrally placed Lombardy poplar, the twin ginko trees, the magnificent planes all add to the arboreal distinction. Sitting in this churchyard, one is aware, at all times, of a sense of the apartness to the place; traffic and people in Tower Bridge Road and Abbey Street seem far away: people busy with jobs are far away from the worries of the unemployed, of the self-employed sitting out time in the garden of rest.

The former graveyard became overcrowded in the nineteenth century and a memorial at the south entrance records its transfer to the vestry of Bermondsey in 1882, and its opening to the public in 1883, after clearance. Yet the dead have not abandoned us: pinning one's ear to the ground, I believe it possible to hear them still: voices babbling with mirth and hilarity, voices shrieking with dismay and torment. Is it not possible that the vibrations of all human voices live on? Vibrations which the hypersensitive ear of the creative musician picks up and transforms into a language which unites the living and the dead.

And what of the voices of the living in the churchyard today? Sitting here in the sun, opening my post, adding up my figures, doing my proof reading, I have been sung to, crooks have made their confessions to me. There was the lunatic with the antique chair who one afternoon shouted at me: 'I own this park, I am in charge of the tulips and the foxes, I am the vicar here, I sleep here', and rounded off his performance with notes on a tin whisle pipe.

Above: *South west view of St Mary Magdalene, Bermondsey, as it appeared in the year 1804*: frontispiece to G.W. Phillips' history.

Above: *Abbey house and offices: the property and residence of J. Riley*; a drawing, *c.* 1826 by C. Burton, engraved by P. Simonau.

# WITHIN THE SOUTH LONDON MISSION

Within the courtyard at the South London Mission there are green tubs containing shrubs, roses in large brown square containers, garden plants in troughs and pots on the ledges. Here too is a small glasshouse and a shelter for bicycles.

One January afternoon in 1993 the courtyard filled with seating and people came from all over for the dedication service to mark the completion of the long delayed upper storey of the residential block on three sides of the courtyard. I had been asked to play the hymn tunes on the violin. I made some special musical arrangements; an umbrella was held over me as drizzle started to come down. The old lady organist took my photograph, and gave me a print some weeks later.

Then one day, I looked out of the window and saw that the canoes had come: green, and red, stranded there whale-like, giant pea pods, deposited there for quite some weeks by the scouts from the attached Manor Church in Galleywall Road.

Students live in the residential block: accountancy, criminal law, graphic design, medicine at Guy's Hospital Medical School are their subjects. The medical students were under strain, during their exams last summer: stressed out before, and exhilarated after. 'That's your problem...' a gruff voice from next door suddenly barked out; 'go away, find somewhere else...'. Caught poignantly between very late childhood and early adulthood, their studies are serious and intense; their pleasures are innocent. Deep in their bible-fat text books during the day, they explode with noise and excitement as they eat their evening meals in front of early evening TV football or tennis.

Above: An illustration by Ernest Hasseldine from the South London Mission 1920 annual report entitled: 'God's lighthouse: the story of rescue and redemption in the slums of South London.'

The 2,000 seats were in the Central Hall behind the facade shown, demolished in the 1960's to make way for present day Cluny Place House. Since then services have been held in the converted vestibule.

Above: An illustration by Ernest Hasseldine from the South London Mission 1921 annual report entitled: 'A door of hope: a record of Christian work among the broken and despairing of South London.'

Queues still form today for free food distribution.

# TANNER STREET: Bermondsey old time, new time

Tanner Street, formerly Russell Street, runs from the Bermondsey Street junction eastwards into Jamaica Road, opposite St Saviour's Dock. It is evocative of Bermondsey's past with its mixture of industrial and public buildings and sites, and typical of its present day state with its small service type businesses and residential conversions. At the corner of Bermondsey Street, next to number 109 you will find a previous owner spelt out on the brickwork: Bermondsey Wire Works, William Cockle & Co. Number one, Tanner Street, renovated *CXT House* comes next: a press cuttings agency CXT (the initials stand for nothing!) for corporate clients, employing some 50 staff, operates from here, established in 1988 and now part of public relations company Dewe Rogerson. Numbers three, five and seven, and now renovated, form a terrace of interlinked, converted warehouses, built in 1838. Once occupied by wool merchants James Lord, and at the turn of the century by Simon & Co, perambulator makers, number three is now the home of *Magee Associates*, run by Belinda Magee and Niall Connolly. Niall Connolly has a special attachment to the area: the offices of his graphic design and communications services business are decorated with large scale photographic studies, and his clients receive a special little booklet, with informative text, small photographs and charming wood cut illustrations by Jane Whitaker: *A world of its own*: a walk from Hay's Galleria to Bermondsey Square.

More business activity goes on at *Swan Court*, a 1980's block, with a swan and weather vane at the end of a long, bracketed black pole: *Joseph and Partners* are architects; *Austin Mayhead & Co* are private management consultants to central and local government; *PPCR Associates* (public participation, consultation, research) work on surveys with housing and tenants associations. The *Douglas Jackson Group* are loss adjusters and marine surveyors. Here too are: *Keen Meadows Foods, H & C Building Services, International Aviation Services, European Cleaning Services,* and *Michael Morgan*, wine distributors.

During the summer months, tennis players flock to Tanner Street, to the site of the old Bermondsey workhouse. I recorded my impressions in 1992 as follows:

The tennis players present a curious spectacle: athletic types sprint hither and thither; schoolgirls know they are quite useless; students are keen to keep fit; a father comes in with his basket of green balls and tiny offspring; he taps the balls gently at them across the nets; their rackets are almost as big as they are. A gang of kids with their out-of-work father comes in to kick a ball about; the little girls go off into the bushes and yank out an executive's case; they all swoop on it like greedy little vultures; they pull out all the stuff; was this an executive so despairing of his lot that he simply threw it all away? Simply vanished and never went home again? But today, as the afternoon reaches its peak, the park feels no concern for such brooding matters; two spaniels frolic around, the inner city sparrows hop and flit; many people are away, the student year has closed. I sat here, late one afternoon and read a biographical account of an artist's life: lived out in London in the 1940's and 1950's: full of turbulence and anxiety, of endless crazy goings on, of unsatisfied desires, of excessive sociability, and loneliness, and work commissions pouring in all the time; but now the park has emptied completely; a flag flutters over Turtle & Pearce, banner makers since 1872; but everything has now gone very still...

A council block *Tanner House* lies opposite, and on the corner of the play area, at number 36 you will find the entrance to *S.O. Rowe & Son*, a surviving leather firm. Indeed, a few manufacturing firms are still here: *Turtle & Pearce* are at number 31, and have been here for over 30 years; previously at Duke Street Hill, the firm is run by Patrick and Michael Tripp, and specialises in flags, banners, bunting, flagpoles, and other promotional items. The *Raven at the Tower* pub is on the Tower Bridge Road corner and has an attractive sign.

*Wyatt & Co* are at numbers 67-73, east of Tower Bridge Road and occupy premises erected about 1860. Managing director R. Renton's grandfather bought the tin box manufacturing business (storage and cake tins, trays, waste paper bins) from the Wyatt family in the 1920's. *Walter Coles Ltd* have been in the old warehouse at 47-49 for some thirty years; established in 1959 in Surrey Square, they specialise in polythene packaging.

At *Tanner Place*, numbers 54-58, you find a variety of small businesses: *Juliet Poyser* has been a freelance wedding dress designer for 12 years; *Action Plus* is a well established sports photographic agency; the *Dome Consultancy*, run by Chris Simmonds designs point of sale and advertising materials. *McArther Fry* are illustrators and graphic designers; *James Patterson & Co* is an insurance company. Other businesses come and go as elsewhere. You will often glimpse people leaving late padlocking up such premises, but otherwise you may be completely in the dark as to who is there.

At the Tower Workshops in Riley Road, which runs into Tanner Street, you will find a comparable mix: photographers such as Derek Seward (operating since 1961 and specialising in car photography for advertising), Geoff Franklin, reportage photographer; Derek Greenwood is a model maker: there are printers such as Work of Art, and the City Printing Service, and catering firms such as the Cool Ice Man.

Photographer Derek Rowe is at 1-4 Pope Street. Adjacent is a new, mysterious metal cage-like structure painted green. In fact it is nothing more than a garage.

At the upper end of Riley Road stood the old School Board Russell Street School. The Builder engraving gives a vivid impression of the school when new. Later the Bermondsey centre of Southwark College was here. It closed in 1995, was demolished in May 1998 and the site is now being redeveloped by Bellway Homes (article in Southwark News, February 26, 1998). The attractive old school house at number 12, Pope Street is already a private residence. Such is the ever changing Southwark landscape.

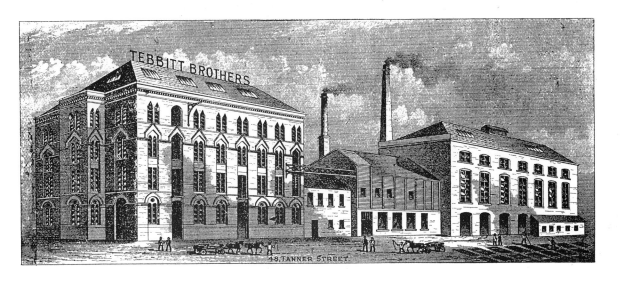

Above: *An engraving of Messrs Tebbitt Bros' Leather Manufactory*, 48 Tanner Street, from A Descriptive Account of Southwark & Bermondsey, W.T. Pike, 1894; works established in 1867.

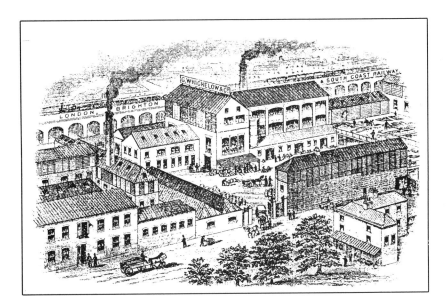

Above: *An engraving of Mr G. Whichelow's Leather Manufactory, Tidal Place, Tanner Street*, from: A Descriptive Account of Southwark & Bermondsey, W.T. Pike, 1894; works established in 1865. Photograph of staff of works in SBR, I.
Thomas Whichelow is buried in Nunhead Cemetary (red granite cross memorial).

*Above: Blue Anchor, Tanner Street* (Jamaica Road end); a watercolour, 1870's, by J.T. Wilson. Courtesy: Southwark Local Studies Library.

Above: *Coopers Arm Tavern*; watercolour drawing by T.H. Shepherd, 1854. Courtesy: Trustees of the British Museum.
There is also a pen and ink drawing, 1837, of this subject by J.C. Buckler.
J.T.Wilson made a watercolour drawing of another Tanner Street pub, the Raven and Sun, in 1870.

Above: *The Tower Bridge Road corner of Tanner Street, with Sarson's vats*; drawing by Martin Millard, 1991. The vats were demolished several years ago, and in 1997 work started on a new residential block (designed by Dransfield architects). Archaeologists did their work and found evidence of the leather trade dating back to the 17th century (article in Southwark News, April 17, 1997).
Another, very different, version of this subject is Vincent Driscoll's oil painting 'Midsummer night'.

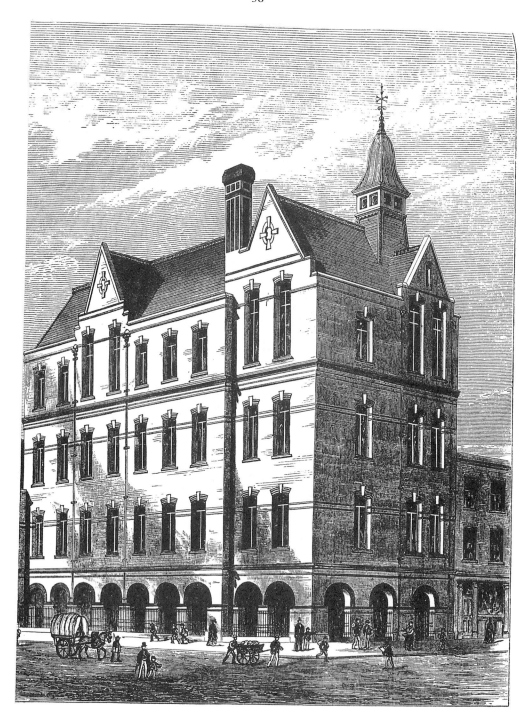

Above: *School Board Schools, Riley Street, Bermondsey,* architect: Joseph James. From The Builder, June 6th, 1874.

39

Above: This strange, historical curiosity is tucked away in the corner of Tanner Street playground. It is all that was preserved of St Olave's Church when demolished in 1928. The site was originally part of vegetable gardens and orchards of the Abbey, later pasture land attached to the farm on Sir Thomas Pope's estate, then market gardens, and later in the second half of the 19th century and early 20th century, the site of St Olave's workhouse (photograph of exterior in SBR, II), demolished in 1925. There are current plans to build a small scale sports hall on part of the childrens' playground area.

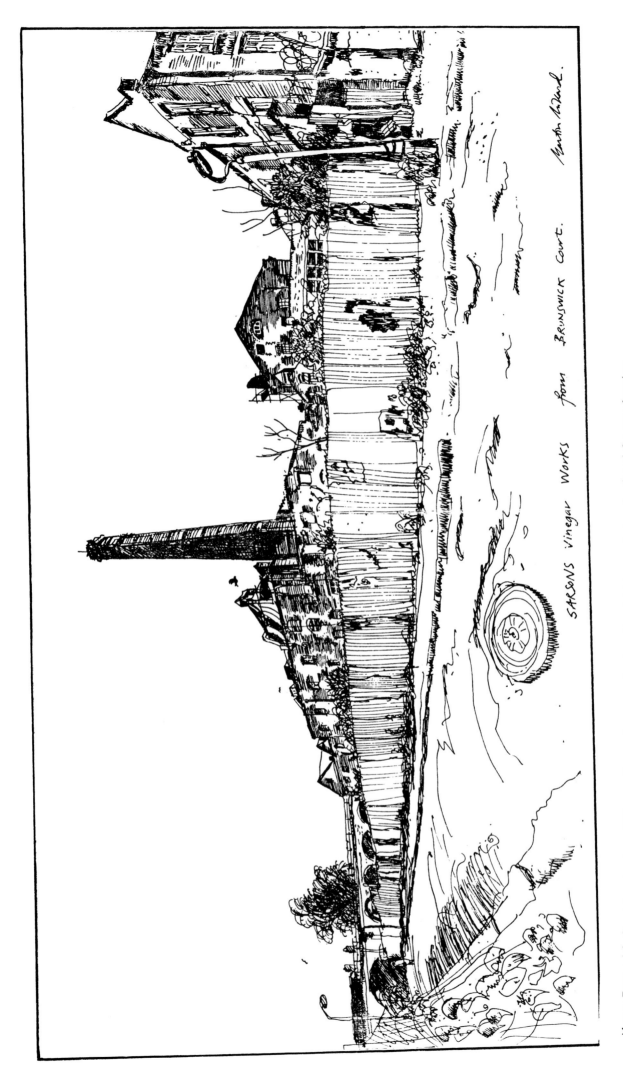

SARSON'S VINEGAR WORKS from BRUNSWICK COURT.

Above: Brunswick Court is a turning off Tanner Street; the vacant land on the right is now being developed for new housing. Sarson's vinegar factory closed in March, 1992; it opened in 1812 and was owned by the Slee family; the company was then taken over by British Vinegars in 1932, and finally bought by Laws Estates.

# BERMONDSEY SIDE STREET: Decima Street

Leading off the bottom end of Bermondsey Street is Decima Street; a side turning of no interest, just like any other all over London, some may say. Yet, my little bedsitter room looks out onto this street, and almost every day I peer out through my window, and watch with never-ending curiosity the ever changing human landscape. On the corner: the Top Quality Fish and Hamburger Bar, a branch of the Handf Group offering housing and finance, and a launderette: places which must provide settings for countless human encounters, for countless human stories if one was to hang around there.

At weekdays this street is full of humanity, full of people on business and doings; from four o'clock in the afternoon onwards endless vans pass through here: removal firms, plumbers, electricians, all kinds of building services, security services, printers, roofing contractors, pest control services; there is no end to the self-employed people here offering specialist services. People doing business with printers pass through here, coming from elsewhere in London and the country; there are medical students intent on their futures, school teachers, social workers, people coming to the job club.

At weekends the street goes very quiet; kids play about with nothing to do, dogs are walked, bored youths trot home with their rented videos, or bottles of booze. Children come to visit their ageing parents, sit about on sofas, wonder where life is; people lean over their balconies, stare into space, try to figure out what life is all about; but nobody can really know what goes on within the rooms of these huge council estates. Many people probably find a refuge here: indeed, tucked away up crumbling staircases, one may find extraordinary people: a distinguished scholar and translator of Russian twentieth century poetry; perhaps artists creating vast panoramas of a nation in its death throes before the turn of the millenium, inventors of genius, brilliant pop musicians, dreaming of stardom, who knows, who knows?

**1997 notes:**

Artists indeed hang out around here: a small side turning on the left, south of the Meakin estate, contains *Decima Studios*, and at number three a new gallery space is being developed, run by three young artists Phil Hunt, Alex Chapple and Matt Andrew. They are open Fridays to Sundays, 12.00 - 6.00pm. Southwark News, February 26th, 1998 reported their opening show. There are more studios at 20-30, Wilds Rents. *Visual Response* is a graphic art business here. In adjacent blocks you find *Argent Building Services*, *Redbird Studios*, and *Richer Sounds* (Hi-fi equipment). Returning to Decima Street there are two printing works: *Spectra Plan Ltd*, *PAC Graphics*, and at numbers 36-38 the *Metropolitan Building Company* in a building dated 1878. Next door is *Sherborne House*, a probation day centre, with two solid blue painted front doors, once a shelter for homeless girls as shown in the illustration below.

Opposite: An illustration from The Doctor, by Barclay Baron, 1952. This club, attached to the *Oxford Medical Mission* was at 38 Decima Street from about 1905-20. By 1908 six clubs were operating from Abbey Street, Wolseley Street, Parker's Row, Bermondsey Street, Decima Street, and Riley Street. Activities included sports, debates and lectures, even bookmaking and violin classes in Abbey Street, with weekly religious services.

Now known as the Oxford and Bermondsey Club (amalgamating the Canterbury and Stansfield clubs), a new building opened in Webb Street in 1983. See Mark Say's historical account *A Century of the OBC*, 1997.

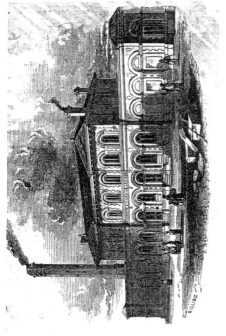

Above: *Bermondsey baths and washhouse*; opened in 1854, the first of their kind in London; adjacent to the town hall, both now demolished. New baths opened in 1927 in Grange Road, and were in use until 1975; now demolished.

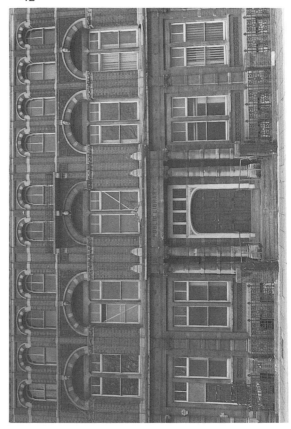

Above: *Old Bermondsey Central Library*; built in 1890; architect: John Johnson. Foundation stone laid by A. Lafone (MP for Bermondsey 1886-92, 1895-90). Two lamps used to stand on the two entrance piers. Building now houses LBS Leisure Services Department.

Above: *Council offices* built 1928; architect: H. Tansley. Note the Bermondsey B.C. coat of arms on the pediment, and the surmounting acroterion. The wrought iron panels continue along the Neckinger Road side of the building.

# SPA ROAD AND BERMONDSEY SPA GARDENS

The Grange Road end of Spa Road was the municipal centre of the old borough of Bermondsey, and London Borough of Southwark services are run from here (and elsewhere) today; the gap between the old library and Tansley's Greek revival style council offices (building design, health and safety departments, etc) was once filled by the Town Hall. Today there is a courtyard area leading to a 'first stop shop' (for advice), and a restaurant; the Woodmill Building behind houses financial services. On the Grange Road corner there is the Alfred Salter Neighbourhood Office. Rumaging in the Local Studies Library one evening, I was interested to alight on a booklet showing interior view of different council departments and their personnel many years ago: *Souvenir of the opening of the new municipal offices, November 1st, 1930*. Large business premises are here too: *Cormorant Electrical Manufacturers and City Guardian electrical contractors*; *Oyez* (a division of the Solicitor's Law Stationery Society), and *West Leigh* (metal windows).

*Bermondsey Spa Gardens* is a pleasant place to go for a stroll – here one can retrieve a sense of relative normality, see things in perspective perhaps; wooden tables and seats are there for picnics; blackbirds bounce about, lost in their own impenetrable realm of being; pigeons are aware of nothing; fathers take their todlers for a stroll; youths puff at cigarettes. Not everyone who strolls about here will be aware of two memorial trees. In the centre of the rose garden a tree of heaven (Ailanthis altissima) was planted recently. A tablet records: "this tree is dedicated to the Bermondsey councillors of old who lined the streets with the trees of heaven to ease the effects of poverty on health and the quality of life and to the working class communities of the borough who withstood great hardship with great fortitude. Others both here and abroad were to follow the councillors' initiative". At the Grange Road end, there is a memorial tree, planted 1956 to the memory of Eveline May Lowe, LL.D., J.P., 1870-1956, 'a true friend of Bermondsey people and a great Londoner.' The original Spa Gardens were flourishing from 1770-1805, and the Local Studies Library has a ground plan drawing, 1803. Thomas Keyse, an artist, was the entrepreneur behind the spa, and one of his descendants Frank Keyse published a booklet history in 1986. The exact site was close to the Rouel Road junction, further north (site of Pearce Duff's factory extension). Keyse Road is a small turning off Grange Road (Southwark's Parks Warden Service occupy the only building).

Spa Road continues past the *Queen's Arms*, past the *Salvation Army* block, with a new *Mowlem* construction training centre in the old factory opposite, past the *Lion pub* on the corner of Enid Street, under the railway viaduct and out into Thurland Road where St James' church rises before us like an astonishing aparition, after all the municipality.

Retracing our steps, Rouel Road leads into the *Dockley Road Industrial Estate*. The housing estate around here contrasts 1960's barrack-like housing blocks with smaller 1980's housing, the brown brickwork, gabled roof tops, balconies and door porches all replying with typical antagonism to the anonymity of the 1960's. There is another small industrial estate nearby in Alscot Road. Number 45 is a small, modern block characterised by a large glass stairway in the centre. On the wall of the vacant plot in Rouel Road someone wrote the message in large letters: 'Good luck, Jane and Liz, Love P, K, and V.' In today's very troubled and uncertain world, there is a poignancy in this buoyant, heartfelt message. It has been there for some years now, but no doubt in time it will vanish.

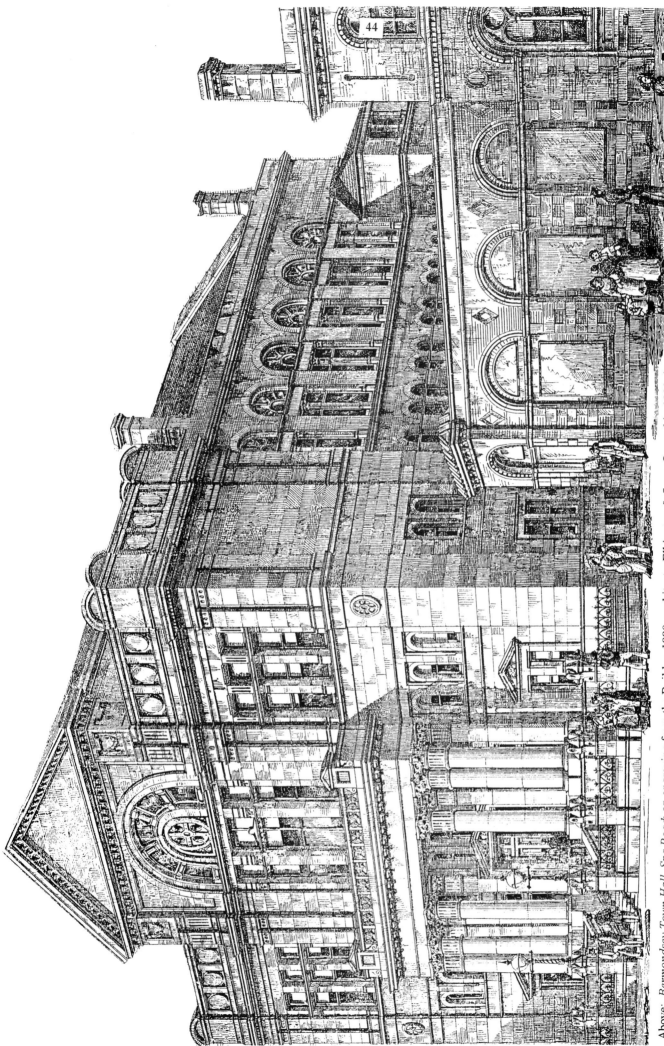

Above: *Bermondsey Town Hall, Spa Road*; an engraving from the Builder, 1880; architects: Elkington & Sons. Opened in 1882, it became a well-known South London public building; destroyed by bombing, the site is now a courtyard space, between the old library and the council offices.

Above: *The commemorative plaque on the wall of Chartes House*, Abbey Street. Another plaque was placed, in 1995, on the wall of houses in the Radcliffe Road block, just east of the White Bear pub.

Above: *Eastern end of Grange Walk*; a drawing by R.J. Angel, 1905; Bermondsey's most ancient, most mysterious corner. Note the surviving gateway hinges (in centre). This drawing was published in the Bermondsey Borough Council *Catalogue of prints and drawings in the Bermondsey Public Libraries*, 1927.

Opposite: *The old charity school in Grange Walk.* Previously owned by St Mary's Magdalene (before 1830 a girls' school ran from a room over the porch there), it was sold recently to Russell Gray (Shiva Ltd) for redevelopment.

# GRANGE WALK

Grange Walk is a quiet, domestic street. Indeed, as we stroll down this turning off Tower Bridge Road, we feel ourselves almost intruders in a very private place of residence. Numbers 5-7, walls painted blue and pink are of medieval origin, and formed one side of the abbey gatehouse (we note the name plaque 'The Gate House' on numbers 6-7). Numbers 8-11 are early eighteenth century, as is number 67 across the road. The rather splendid wrought iron gates, dated 1986 of *Grange House* lead into an entrance way (with offices beyond the courtyard), decorated with Roman style panel murals, and a geometric, patterned ceiling. The new housing, by way of contrast, seems mean, unlovable, and discordant in these ancient surroundings, old houses with door hoods, shutters and attic windows.

The old charity school is dated 1830, the adjacent house on the other side of Griggs Place is dated 1896 and the terrace 1890; contrasting with the pre-war *Aylwin Estate* opposite (named after Aylwin Child, who founded the priory, later Bermondsey Abbey, in 1082).

On the corner of Fendall Street we note the converted *Grange Walk Infants School*, 1853, with two modern, sequestered corner houses, forming *Grange Walk Mews*; opposite is *Melford Court* with port-hole windows, and wrought iron stairways leading to first floor entrances: property developments of the 1980's, and naturally all strictly private places. The new housing block at number 41 comes as a surprise: a mediterranean style intrusion, variegated brickwork, decorative green balconies in the central section, roofs at three levels with white brackets, and a large inner courtyard behind a locked gate. It has a kind of tactful, and not disharmonious presence in this old street, and leads us on to other large blocks: *St Vincent House, Valois House* (named after Catherine de Valois, widow of Henry V, and banished to the abbey, and *Woodville House* (named after Elizabeth Woodville, widow of Edward IV, sent here in 1486). Balconies of these blocks have been recently painted: purple, green and plum red. Further down the road to the right: *Larnaca House*, and *George Tingle House*. *Mabel Goldwin House* is headquarters of the Social Services Department of the council (Mabel Goldwin was a councillor 1949-86, and mayor 1971-2). It lies between *Evelyn Coyle House* (a council day centre for the elderly with mental health problems), and Larnaca Works, where there are artists' studios.

The lower end of Grange Walk was once known as Horney Lane. Here, opposite the old council blocks, you will find new housing to the left, built by Barratt's in the early 1990's for the South London Family Housing Association: tiny gardens, little porches, small yellow balconies, attached to supporting long yellow columns.

Above: *A new residential block*, built in the late 1980's, at number 41, Grange Walk.

Above: *Neckinger Mills*; a water-colour painting by C.J. Buckler, 1826. Originally occupied by Neckinger Paper Mills (on the banks of the Neckinger stream), and from 1802 by Bevington's tannery; site acquired by the council in 1936. The Joanna Southcott chapel stands in the centre. Courtesy: Southwark Local Studies Library.

# ABBEY STREET

ABBEY STREET named not unnaturally after Bermondsey Abbey, was laid out in 1820; it passes from St Mary's churchyard, through the tunnel of the railway viaduct, and out into Jamaica Road. If today it has a dull, aching boredom about it, then it must be because much has gone from it: Dockhead House (part of the Time and Talents Association), the Oxford Medical Mission, the Star Music Hall, for example. Frederick Moody illustrated the Star Music Hall in his London In Pen & Ink series (What's on in London, July 19, 1961). An eighteenth century painting (reproduced in the Bermondsey Labour Magazine, January 1927) shows the old Star Tavern in a rural setting, and a 1937 photograph appears in SBR. Founded in 1867, it became a cinema in 1919 and since 1939 was a warehouse. The Bevington tannery was established in 1802 on the site of a former paper mill, now occupied by Neckinger Estate. The building in Abbey Street dates from 1864. The firm moved from here some years ago and Matthew Goldsmith acquired the property in 1979. He operates his picture restoration business from here, and has an international clientele; he rents the rest of the building out to other artists (see article in South London Press, February 27th, 1998, Focus on a firm series). The building looks especially impressive when viewed from the Arnold Estate to the north.

The Fleece pub on the corner of Neckinger Road is another impressive old building, with ten pilasters at ground floor level. Paint can brighten any dull street and in recent years balconies, panels and doors of council blocks have been painted: *Breton House*, red; *Marlow House*, blue; *Rufus House*, orange. The old terraces on the southern side have also had a face lift of green paint.

*The Beormund Community Centre* (named after Beormund, the Saxon Lord, and origin of the place name) stands on the corner of Druid Street and runs educational, recreational and sports classes and sessions. In the entrance foyer you will find six large historical photomontages, showing local scenes (made by Nicky May).

In DRUID STREET you find small businesses under the arches: car services mainly, but here too are: the *Display Board Company Ltd*, the *South London Timber Company*, The three large gates of *Pallet Services* look ominous and the street's mystery is enhanced by the three railway tunnels at Gedling Place, Millstream Road and Tanner Street. Opposite, to the north lies the Arnold Estate and on the corner of Sweeny Crescent the *Marquis of Wellington* pub. Close by is the *Fisher Downside Club*, built in 1973, a boys' club famous for its boxing; Steve Hiser has been a coach here since 1973 (article in Southwark News, May 11th, 1995). The club is currently appealing for £1.3 million for repair and modernisation work to the building (article in South London Press, May 1st, 1998). There are more tunnels at the western end of Druid Street: Roper Lane, Brunswick Court, White's Ground and Crucifix Lane all lead into Druid Street through these dark, chilling underpasses. South of Tooley Street you find the premises of *Bermondsey Scrap Metal* and *South London Plastering Merchants*, but the street ends on an altogether different note with the offices of the St Olave's and Bermondsey United Charities at numbers 6-8 (upper storey added in 1996), with a 1794 milestone outside. The King of Belgium pub lies opposite, and we are now in an altogether different locality.

ENID STREET lies on the other side of the road and foot tunnel; it has a few more automobile and drink warehousing businesses, and then peters out and the arches at the eastern end stand unused. The street is bleak and hardly a place for a pleasurable promenade. Yet, a solitary tree of heaven with small sapling trees at its base stands at the centre. Opposite, to the south, lies the Neckinger Estate and a children's playground. Children were playing there, even though it was a cold December evening when I was there. This is home for them...the chimney of the old factory nearby, the trains passing overhead...however bleak their landscape may be, the children of the world play on.

49

Opposite: *Memorial to Violet Alice Tritton* (died in 1957) on the wall of Bromleigh House, off Abbey Street; unveiled in September 1959, and executed by students from Camberwell School of Arts & Crafts. She was a much loved and respected worker at the Dockhead branch of the Time and Talents Association for many years. Dockhead House at 225, Abbey Street, opened in 1931 and was demolished in 1957.

There were also premises at 79, Abbey Street, 1913-41.

Above: A drawing from 'The Doctor', by Barday Baron, 1952. One of the earliest buildings of the *Oxford Medical Mission*, established by Dr John Stansfield in 1897.

Above: A drawing from folding leaflet *Bermondsey Walk*, 1984. Courtesy: London Borough of Southwark.

The drawings above and below give a long range perspective of the subject; David Fried's drawing by contrast, shows the artist zooming in with dramatic effect on a close-up study of one part of the structure.

Opposite: Drawing, 1835, of the *London to Greenwich viaduct* crossing Abbey Street.

Above: One of the two foot tunnels (with road for traffic in between), held up by cast iron columns, at the far end of *Abbey Street*. There is another similar tunnel at the end of Spa Road.

Above: *St Paul's Church and School*, Kipling Street (off Long Lane); from the Illustrated London News, 1848; architect: Samuel Sanders Teulon; demolished in 1963. The architect also designed St Stephen's, nearby in Manciple Street; also St Mark's, Silvertown, and St Stephen, Rosslyn Hill, Hampstead. 1935 photograph of church and vicinity in SBR, II.

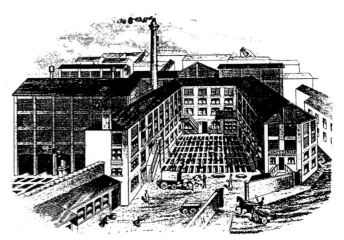

Above: *Messrs. James Garnar's Leather Manufactory*, The Grange; an engraving from A Descriptive Account of Southwark & Bermondsey, W.T. Pike, 1894.

Above: A drawing, 1812, of the *Grange farmhouse*, which belonged to the Abbey, and provides the origin of the street names The Grange, Grange Road, and Grange Walk.

# LONG LANE, AND ENVIRONS

LONG LANE leads out of central Bermondsey into Borough High Street, culminating with the majestic presence of St George the Martyr, as seen from its eastern end. Although dreary, monotonous, it has its points of interest, with intriguing side turnings. Not quite a High Street, it has its share of shops and pubs: *Simon the Tanner* at number 231, the old *Ship* at 228 (now converted into flats), *the George* at number 111, are the pubs. There are food places: *Britannia Pizza and Pasta* next door to the George, *Fresh Bite/Chez la Mama* (a nice alternative name!) at 89a, with *George's fish bar* next door, and opposite the *Long Lane fish bar*, and a *Costcutter* supermarket. Florists *Flowers by Wells* is at number 158. The biggest retail commercial establishment at present is the *antiques emporium* at number 237. This 1950's building was at one time a factory, later owned by TSB for cheque printing; several years ago Trinity College of Music was thinking of moving here. Tim Pomroy of Callington Estates who owned the building in the 1990's considers that eventually it will be turned into apartments, offices and shops. At present it is an exciting place in which to wander and look. South London Press featured one trader *Paul Lebreton* in their Focus on a Firm series on February 6th, 1998; 'Bermondsey has got so much history, it has more antiques than anywhere else in England. It's the world's best kept secret', he observed.

Council blocks came to the lane with redevelopments in the 1930's-50's (there is an early twentieth century block at number 102), but there is still a nineteenth century presence, especially at the lower end. The old Hepburn and Gale leather warehouse of about 1875 has a dominating presence at number 239. Now known as *Tanners Yard* its windows are lit up at night time as very rich people settle into their new apartments. The firm merged with Samuel Barrow (factory in the Grange) in 1920, and you can read an account of the enterprise in a book published in 1948, *Everything in leather: the story of Barrow Hepburn and Gale Ltd*, written by Dennis Bardens. Nearby at number 217 is an old stable complex, 1886, architect J. Butterworth, with house at street level. The premises are owned and occupied by *Profot*, a photographic laboratory, with the House of Colour and the Cable Shop at the rear end. Mounting blocks survive at the western wall, and with only a little imagination we feel ourselves transported to a slower, more human age. Across the road is another old warehouse block, now *St Christopher's House*, a hostel for Guy's Hospital medical students. Opposite are the warehouses of Larderfresh and Puritan Maid Ltd.

Long Lane also has its *mercurial demon sprinter*: if you are here in the evenings around 8.00pm, or 5.00pm you might glimpse the demon librarian runner, sprinting away home after another day at the Local Studies Library. He dreams perhaps of his ancestral past when hasty delivery was required for urgent messages to the powers that be. He sprints away in his red or blue long pants, whilst everyone else lumbers slowly along.

Perambulating any main street in London means glimpsing endless side turning we could stray into, never quite knowing what we will find. Westom Street runs to the north and south of Long Lane. At the corner, by the pub *Valentine's* (see South London Press, February 13th, 1998), with the *Tabard Gardens Tenant Management Co-op* building adjacent, we glimpse the Leathermarket small business complex. Across the road is the old Lord Wellington pub; *Wing Hing Chinese take away* now occupies part of the building.

In KIPLING STREET (formerly Nelson Street) there are two old pubs: *The Britannia*, and *Guy's Arms. Coppen and Healey*, musical instrument dealers and repairers were operating from number 50 for some years; now John Coppen Woodwind is at unit 7, Leathermarket, and Mr Healey, stringed instruments, has moved to Sutton.

In CROSBY ROW we encounter the Rainbow building and St Hugh's part of the *Charterhouse Mission*, built 1892-8, architects: Carpenter and Ingelow. An interior drawing of the church was published in the Daily Graphic, February 7th, 1895; there was a centenary celebratory Open Day here on 5th February, 1998. Wandering around here, it is likely that we will stop in our tracks quite suddenly when we encounter the truncated *mural by Peter Pelz* of an ascended Christ on the Purlock Street side of the establishment. Painted in 1976 it aroused considerably controversy on account of the nudity and the uppermost part was obliterated, with plans to replace the work with a new mural describing the activities within the building. Twenty years on, the truncated version remains...Close by is *Purlock Hall*, a London Borough of Southwark inner city teacher education centre. There is more of Charterhouse in a building next to the Whitesmith's Arms: the Ark Playgroup and women's project. Behind St Hugh's, and overlooking Long Lane is the *Beormund 'special' school*. Straying into the courtyard we are jerked forwards in time when we encounter the space age murals there.

53

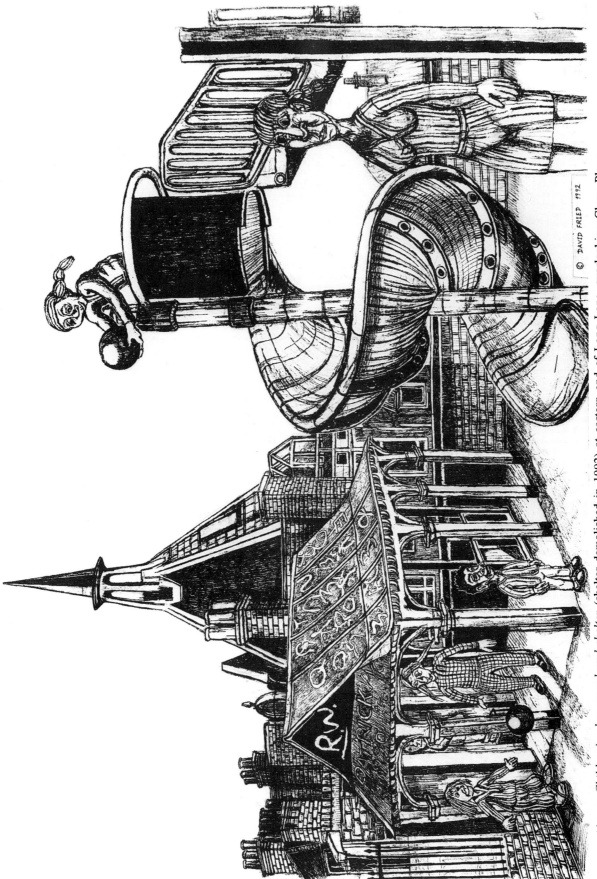

Above: *Children's playground and shelter* (shelter demolished in 1992) at eastern end of Long Lane, overlooking Cluny Place (turret of the South London Mission in the background). A plaque on the wall overlooking Cluny Place records that this was a quaker burial ground from 1696 until its closure in 1855. A few gravestones remain in the eastern corner. SBR, I has a 1934 photograph of the site, a very different slide, with different looking young and old people, and the drinking fountain (now gone too).

In Crosby Row there are two intruiging side places: *Plantain Place* with its two attractive 1908 gate houses, and further north *Baden Place*, dominated by a tall white clock tower (containing a lift), renovated for office use. Here you will find a variety of businesses concerned with office-based activities such as public relations, accountancy and finance. At ground floor level you find the *International Arts Bureau*. I was there late one evening and the managing director, Rod Fisher, was still busy filing documents. I spoke to him through the door, reminded him of our brief acquaintance some twenty years ago. What happens to people over such a long period of time? Earlier that week I had met someone at a concert at Conway Hall, likewise not seen for many years. Inevitably, time wears people down, people look more crumpled, less youthful, yet the personality, the timbre and accent of voice remain unchanged. Rod Fisher, when information officer at the Arts Council had a dream, the dream of an arts beaurocrat perhaps, but he longed to bring an international dimension into the work of his organisation, and in 1994 he went freelance on contract to his former employer. That evening he told me he had never been working so hard as at present; he pointed to his tray overflowing with correspondence, the bulging bookshelves, told me of the theft of his computers, and the current uncertainty of future funding, perhaps leaving only himself in charge; and yes, there was competition, he was in a field others wanted to enter, sensing rightly or wrongly that it was a lucrative one. He has recently started a new information bulletin called *Navigator*, taking one through the complexities of European funding, legislation, networks and structures. On his desk there lay proofs for the next issue; behind on the wall hung a print of a Miro painting; a box of chocolate biscuits lay open nearby. Alone in his office, late that night, it occurred to me that this was the world of the entrepreneur in a nutshell: driven by a sense of vision, forever moving forward, prodigiously hard working and ambitious, yet too often ignored by the outer wide world. 'Is there anyone there?' must be the cry of many an entrepreneur all alone, late at night.

There are more businesses at *Gallery Court*, two three-storeyed blocks, with roof top elevations slanted just very slightly, in Pilgrimage Street and in Hankey Place. The headquarters of Richer Sound PLC (audio and hi-fi specialists retailers) are here; other operations run from 20, Wilds Rents. The curved metal sign with red circle decorating both buildings suggest at first that art galleries hang out here, but no so, currently. The *Selected Rug and Matting* is on the corner at number 74, Long Lane, managing director: Mr Eisenberg. This is the site of the old Southwark Wire Works, established in 1824. Also currently in this building are *Quadrant Design Associates, Hart Ryan Productions*, and until very recently *Hilfe Ltd*, which specialises in economical and political analysis of overseas countries for British banks.

Close by, on the corner of Manciple Street we discover to our delight a small rose garden: *Hankey Place Garden*: a place in which to sit quietly, much our lunchtime sandwiches, and try to get into perspective one's abiding sense of a world on the edge...

Above: the truncated, half obliterated mural by Peter Pelz in Porlock Street, off Long Lane.

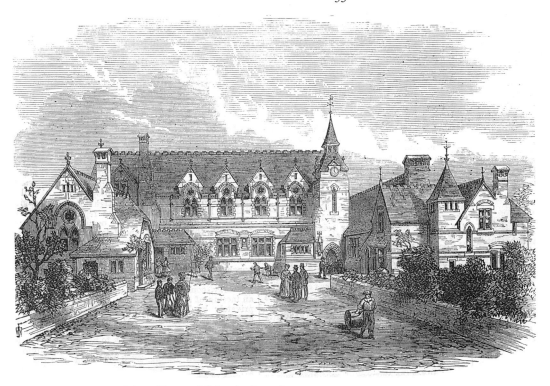

Above: *St Mary Magdalene National Schools*; from the Illustrated London News, 1872; now known as the Boutcher School commemorating its founder William Boutcher (of the leather factors Boutcher, Mortimore & Co).

Above: *Old Bacon's School*: a watercolour drawing by T.H. Shepherd, 1852; Courtesy: Trustees of the British Museum. School built in 1718, today's building erected in 1890; now part of Southwark College.

Opposite: The Grange Road entrance to the Alaska housing complex; note the ornamental tusks (also used in the Bacon Grove railings). The factory building of today was erected in 1932, architects: Wallis, Gilbert and Partners. Martin's fur factory was here and you can read their history in *Under eight monarchs: C.W. Martin & Sons Ltd, 1823-1953.*

# GRANGE ROAD/SOUTHWARK PARK ROAD

GRANGE ROAD can be perambulated with interest, from its junction with Tower Bridge Road, up to Bermondsey Spa Gardens, and its continuation as Southwark Park Road: old and new terraces, old houses, pubs, schools, cafes.

In 1997 there was a major redevelopment and conversion project: the former Southwark Council Education Offices building was turned over to residential use: now known as *Tower View Court*, this Barratt project has found ready purchasers for all its exorbitantly priced flats. Week by week, the bricks were piled up, new windows and doors went into the frame of the old building; then lumps of stone arrived, flower beds were planted in the entrance, the sales office opened and new people now live here. *Tower Mansions* was built in the early 1990's, a terrace at numbers 80-87. The old *Alaska* factory building, renovated by Charterhouse Estates originally for business use in 1991 is now a residential block: its courtyard is a grandiose approach to home; and the Bellway Homes development *Trocette Mansion* now straddles Tower Bridge Road, and the bottom end of Bermondsey Street. Scrutinising all these newcomers, often very young people, one may conclude that these are all people into big money from one source or another, people whose roots are not here and who may not in fact live here very much at all; in fact, they all seem to be saying: we are here to keep you out, we are in no way part of you...was I become a little too paranoid, I wondered? So I asked my fish and chip man whether he was meeting the newcomers in his shop. He beamed at me, as normally, 'very intelligent people,' he commented, 'not at all snobbish; doctors, dentists, city folk, people like that...'

Pubs too are being converted, have new owners, or are currently boarded up. *Sansom's* on the corner of Griggs Place is a fine, swaggering building dated 1898, with decorative gables and a tall corner chimney, and it is now owned by Rosecall & Co, an American law firm. The *Earl of Derby* on the corner of Fendall Street is now being converted; the *Red Cow*, on the corner of the Grange, and the *Royal George* in Abbey Street are both boarded up at present. 'The end of the old fashioned boozer?' asks Southwark News,October 31st, 1996. Then turn to the recently launched Southwark Local section of the South London Press, and week after week you find profile articles on successful, old and newly established pub businesses, those managers and entrepreneurs who have found the winning formula. Just opposite the Alaska, you find the thriving *Final Furlong*, a large place, full of racing memorabilia, providing lots of entertainment, a wide-ranging menu, and beer garden in the Grange. The *Grange pub* opposite Keyse Road is also a thriving and popular establishment. *The Fort*, on the corner of Alscot Road is now under new management as a gay pub. The sign has gone, the walls are now painted black and deep blue, and the windows are kept discreetly shuttered.

Then there are cafes: The *Tasty Cafe* at number 211; the *Grange Cafe* at 188; and the *Wizard of Oz* at 163-4.

Old school buildings are here: the o*ld Bacon's School*, rebuilt in 1891 is a striking landmark with its turret and gables, entrance piers surmounted by alcove from the old earlier building. The bust of Josiah Bacon by William Cox is now at Bacon's College of Technology in Surrey Docks. The *Boutcher School*, built 1872, architect: Joseph Gale, is set back considerably from the road and could easily be overlooked, but it is an attractive building, as conveyed by the reproduced engraving - gabled windows and small towers. The *Kintore Way Nursery School* is a much more recent establishment.

Domestic housing dates from the last century: on the northern side the terrace, 1896; and numbers 8-11, and number 44, early nineteenth century. Number 44 is conspicuous for its porch and ionic columns.

*Bermondsey Health Centre*, 1936, architect: H. Tansley (who designed the council offices in Spa Road in an altogether contrasting syle) is an important establishment in the history of public health in the area.

At the junction with Dunton Road, Grange Road becomes SOUTHWARK PARK ROAD. We pass the wrought iron gates of *Aylwin School* (featured in South London Press, schools report series, March 6th, 1998) and the *Rose and Crown* pub on the corner of Alma Grove; beyond there are attractive terraces: Court, Myrtle, Lilly and Rose cottages. In Monnow Road we find an old London School Board building, now *Spa School*, with attractive school house building, and at the Southwark Park Road junction there is the *Queen Victoria* pub (profiled in South London Press, February 27th, 1998). More large pub buildings follow on: the *Blue Anchor* on the corner of Blue Anchor Lane, and the *Ancient Foresters* at the top of Galleywall Road.

As Southwark Park Road forks to the north, we might care to stray into Raymouth Road (*Raymouth Arms* pub on the corner), to visit the *Pot Company*, the yellow painted walls advertising a wide range of imported wares. The business, established in 1985, is run by Kevin McMahon, a former landscape gardener, and operates a wholesale operation to the trade and its franchised shops, with a small retail shop at Raymouth Road.

At number 351, Southwark Park Road is *Bede House*, a community and educational centre, with premises also in Abbeyfield Road. It can trace its origins back to the Princess Marie Louise Settlement in Jamaica Road established in 1907. It moved to the present day premises in 1938, an old bakery, and adopted a new name after the Venerable Bede, to denote its Christian background. A booklet *The History of Bede House 1938-88*, by Susanna Watson is available. One of its current educational concerns is to train people with learning difficulties in cookery, and in 1997 a related recipe book (priced £17.50) was published.

Beyond the Bede Centre lie the old *St Andrews Presbyterian Church* (now a Christ Apostolic Church), the attractive *Southwark Park School* (two relief friezes on the street facade show mother and children), and two pubs, the *Southwark Park Tavern* and the *Stanley Arms*.

To conclude this perambulation, one could take a rest in the Ada Salter Rose Garden in Southwark Park, munch some food, and watch the variegated Southwark humanity pass through on the lakeside pathway.

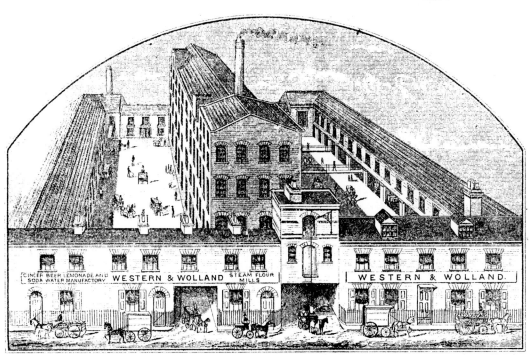

GINGER BEER LEMONADE AND SODA WATER MANUFACTORY — WESTERN & WOLLAND STEAM FLOUR MILLS — WESTERN & WOLLAND.

# WESTERN & WOLLAND,

## 69, 70 & 71, Grange Walk,
## and 211, Grange Road,

# BERMONDSEY.

# PAGES WALK/CRIMSCOTT STREET/BRICKLAYERS ARMS

PAGES WALK is an evocative name, recalling perhaps the proximity of the Bricklayers Arms station, built in 1844 as a terminus for the Croydon and South East Railways. Used later for goods trains, it closed in 1980. The 1967 flyover development destroyed much of the area including the pub that gave its name to the station, as well as the Old Kent Road public library opposite.

*The Bricklayers Arms Distribution Centre*, built in 1991, is now on the site in MANDELA WAY, with other business blocks. It is a chilling, alienating environment today, a place of paper and officialdom: a long, broken strip of brick facades, with corrugated metal sides, and sinister large gates, the forecourts targeted tall green lamps and video cameras. Paper merchants Howard Smith, Contract Papers, Dixon and Roe, Thom and Cook are based here. Opposite lies a *Metropolitan Police Stores*, and in a building of the same shape offices of the *Royal Mail*. Reader: I go there almost every Friday morning to collect my PO Box mail. The work at the sorting office never ends, it will go on and on for ever. Beyond is the warehouse structure of *Viking Direct*, and a similar one-storey block is occupied by *Mowlem*; there is another low rise, brown brick block further down the road, occupied by the *Stationery Office/ Parliamentary Press* and opposite lies *DNDS*, newspaper distributors, with two metal drums on either side of a brick structure in Dunton Road.

Retracing ones steps, and reduced, understandably to some anxiety, it is a pleasure to plunge back into the nineteenth century world of PAGES WALK: a long terrace, numbers 47-103 with doors and shutters painted in a variety of colours; and at the upper end you find the blank, arcaded wall of the former mid-nineteenth century stables (23 blank arcades, 3 arcades with windows). The *Old Bacon's School*, overlooking the Old Kent Road, of 1896, has now been converted into private flats (School House). Number 110 is an attractive school gate house with a tall chimney. The old school has two turrets, gables and is three-storeyed with characteristic tall windows. In the vicinity there are 1980's developments: such as *Quadrangle Court* and *Tower Walk*. To the north lies the 1976 *Guiness Trust Estate* and beyond *Harold Estate* with an attractive forecourt open space, and the *Creasy Estate* with its hidden patches of grass and trees. It is a pleasure to discover the *Victoria pub* at number 70 (with, rather unusually a Penny Black as a sign). Opposite, on the corner of Willow Walk are the premises of *H.W. Cooper*, glass merchants, and next door the *Sapphire Laundry*.

CRIMSCOTT STREET runs parallel to Pages Walk. It is the site of the first scientific botanic garden established by William Curtis in 1771 who began publishing his 72 part Flora Londiensis here. *Crosse and Blackwell's* pickles factory was here in the first part of the century (photograph in SBR, I), and today the street still has a strong commercial flavour: to the left, on the old factory site is the large *Rich Industrial Estate: Law Society Archives, Hayward Bros* (wine), *Davis Shipping, Acorn Self-storage* are some of the current names on the board outside. In smaller buildings we find printing firms, and food and catering businesses: *F.E. Berman, Benwell Sebard, Ashdown Press* printers; the *Huge Cheese Company, R.S. Ashby*, and *J.D. Link* (established in 1875) catering suppliers.

At the Grange Road corner there is *Lena Fox House*, a hostel for young people, and managed by Shaftesbury Homeless Service. This was formerly the site of the *Bermondsey Medical Mission for Women*, initiated by Doctor Selina Fox in 1904. The Local Studies Library has a booklet on her, 1871-1958, and its annual reports 1931-59. Opposite, next to the garage is number one, Crimscott Street, an old private house, mysterious and isolated.

I did my tour of inspection one cold, damp Sunday afternoon; a weekend when my telephone had gone kaputt. I returned home feeling that I must be living in one of the most lonely, spiritless places on earth. It took me several hours for me to retrieve myself, yet I had gone barely beyond my doorstep.

Above: *Bricklayers Arms Station*: watercolour drawing by Albert J. Jefferys, 1930. Courtesy: South London Gallery.

Above: An engraving from *A Descriptive Account of Southwark and Bermondsey*, W.J.Pike, 1894.

# TOOLEY STREET AND ENVIRONS

Tooley Street is North Southwark's 'High Street', and a civilised reply to the edifices of the hard city across the river. It reminds us of the powers that be, but not overwhelmingly: at the Tower Bridge Road junction, to the east of the old Tower Bridge Hotel stands the *Magistrate's Court* (with police station next to it). Its central facade is august and imposing, its broken, curved pediment revealing a royal coat of arms, and below a curved balcony above the four entrance level pillars. Further down the street at number 283 there is the equally imposing, but friendlier, less inscrutable old St Olave's Union offices, with three gables and dormer windows. This converted residential block forms a part of Millenium Square. A board has been preserved in the entrance listing guardians of the old institution.

To the west lies a branch of the National Westminster Bank, 1900, with an imposing entrance and dome. Behind, *Samuel Bevington*, first mayor of Bermondsey, has a dominating presence on his high plinth, the railings bearing the crest of the former Bermondsey council. *Ernest Bevin*, the trade union leader and politician, by way of contrast, is only a bust and faces southwards. Horas sculpted by E. Whitney-Smith, 1955. Across the road is the old grammar school, now part of Lambeth College. All this municipal dignity and public worthiness dates from almost a century ago.

Large, old pubs are here too: the *King's Arms*, established in 1880 on the corner of Three Oak Lane, and westwards the *King of Belgium* (formerly the King of Prussia), on the corner of Druid Street, with *St John's Tavern* opposite; the *Shipwrights Arms* near the Bermondsey Street junction contrasts with the massive South Eastern Railway offices nearby; the *Antigallican*, established in 1789 on the corner of Vine Lane, and the *Duke of Clarence* on the corner of Battle Bridge Lane are smaller premises. The *Cafe Dell'Ugo* (next to *On Your Bike*), *The Cooperage* and *Sinkers* (both Davy's), all close to the London Dungeon (Southwark's number one tourist attraction) are modern-day establishments. The *Music Cafe* is at 1, Duke Street Hill in Colechurch House.

Several public institutions have now gone: *St Olave's public library* (photograph in SBR, II) stood on the corner of Potters Fields from 1902 until 1970 (on the site of St Anne's Girls Charity School); the old *Public Institute* (see Southwark Annual illustration) was at the top of Fair Street, and the old *Workhouse* stood in Druid Street (then Parish Street) from 1725 until 1922 (occupying the site of the old Artillery Hall).

Potters Fields Park has been extended in recent years – opening up access to the riverside (where Pickle Herring Street previously lay), opposite the Tower of London, and to Butlers Wharf on the other side of Tower Bridge. One can come here to gawp at these monuments, or else to savour the humanity to be found here. I noted in 1992: Down and outs hold out their hands to all and sundry; they beg for pennies; what do the city gents have to say to them? One even managed to scrounge a sandwich off me. Never-ending tourists, in groups, whole gangs, couples, families all stroll through here; they must be many miles away from home; what do they see here? What will they remember about this place? And the city folk: what are they thinking of, as they strut along bolt upright; groups of young men who are making it, solitary university graduates just starting in the city, executives with their secretaries; people from Southwark Crown Court, all pass to and fro here, office workers tired out by a morning's futility come here to puff at a cigarette, and escape into a book. I too often sit there munching my lunch-time sandwiches, fed up with my morning efforts, feeling distracted, wondering about my future, wondering who on earth is going to come around the corner next; but this is certainly not a lunch-time parade of Bermondsey folk.

Returning to Tooley Street: at number 150 we find London's only Peruvian restaurant *Fina Estampa*, run by Bianca and Richard Jones; at number 148 Magdalen House has offices of graphic art services; at numbers 112-114 are offices of *Eilers and Wheeler*, importers and distributors of dairy produce; at number 108 is the *London Bridge Dental Practice*; at numbers 92-94 the *Psychosynthesis and Education Trust* provides qualifications in counselling and psychotherapy, and at number 90 there is the *Great Wall Chinese restaurant*: a curious, yet not untypical mix of contemporary businesses.

Above: *Disi Lisi Teapots*: a stall in Hays Galleria (no longer trading), run by John Foster and Elizabeth Palmer. Their newsletter No 1, November 1991 records: 'On All Fools Day this year we abandoned our secure employments to seek greater life fulfilment by addressing our ambition to trade in British, handmade, novelty teapots.'

Above: *Hostel for down and outs in Tooley Street* (now demolished); drawing, 1991, by Martin Millard. Described in Tony Wilkinson's book *Down and Out*, Quartet, 1981.

Opposite: *Fire in Tooley Street*; from the Illustrated London News, 1851.
This fire commenced in basement of No 5, Duke Street, premises of hop factors Wigan, White & Co. The bigger, more famous Tooley Street fire was in 1861, London's biggest since the 1666 fire.

62

Above: *Brewers Arms in Morgans Lane*: watercolour by J. Appleton, 1890. Courtesy: Southwark Local Studies Library.

In *Magdalen Street* to the south you find offices of *Upstage Theatrical Events*, an unusual organisation which offers themed events for corporate companies with its own production company. At numbers 14-24 you find *Langley Systems Ltd*, specialising in automatic doors, and at number 26 on the ground floor of Lion Court, the *Tokei Martial Arts Club*, now in new, purpose-built premises. Local amateur boxer John Prescott started a martial arts club over the Havelock Arms in Fort Road in 1969, moving to Magdalen Street in 1981. Toby Prescott, a cab driver, now runs the club which he regards as the only purpose-built centre of its kind in Britain (article in Southwark News, July 31st, 1997).

Nearby in Shand Street, under the railway line, arch five, you find the *Club Innocence* (formerly Happy Jax), with a striking orange star sign in Crucifix Lane.

Shopping malls are 1980's developments, and Tooley Street has a most grandiose one in the restored Hays Wharf Dock, *Hays Galleria*. The original warehouses were built by Sir William Cubbitt, completed in 1857, and rebuilt after the Tooley Street 1861 fire. The conversion – residential and office accommodation over ground floor shops, welded steel columns supporting the arched glass roof was carried out in 1986 by Michael Twigg Brown and Partners. With its monumental sculpture The Navigators and open-air entertainments, it is a successful and popular development of its period, its shops celebrating food and drink, art and books, fashion and designer products. *Kwan Thai* restaurant opened recently on the river front, a cool restrained interior, contrasting *Hornimans at Hays* bar opposite (article in South London Press, March 20th, 1998), with its gregarious crowds and costal murals. Jose Naranjo has been running his *Sunshine Gallery* at unit 20 since 1996, having previously had a sandwich bar at Tower Hill. His stock is populist and colourful. When there some months ago, I spotted a good rendition of the Navigators by a one A. Bassas, and scenes painted in acrylic by local artist Barbara Everley. Sylvia Ridgewell is another successful entrepreneur and she has been running her up-market *Riverside Bookshop* nearby for some ten yeas, opening a second shop at Shad Thames several years ago. There are unusual gift shops here too: as you enter the Tooley Street block you find Elaine Thompson's *Christmas Shop* opened in 1988 (an American idea). Her recent press release reports: 'new for 1997 is an animated Christmas tree which talks and sings Christmas songs whenever you approach it.' *Pinocchio* is one of six shops selling pine furniture, gifts and toys, owned by the St Martin's Property Corporation. *Obsessions* is also part of a small chain of shops in London, established some ten years and selling a wide range of unusual gifts. Believing that to shop means excitement, it specialises in changing theatrical style presentations.

More businesses are to be found below ground, which takes you from under the Cotton's Centre to Price Waterhouse. You can be informed at the *Southwark Tourist Information Centre*, where you will find a wide-ranging stock of local interest books and many publicity leaflets, run by the energetic and ambitious Heike Herbert. You can eat at *Bella Pasta*, be groomed and beautified at the *Ginger Group*, be serviced at *Scarpa Dry Cleaning and Heel Bar*, and be trimmed and toned in the gym, squash courts, swimming pool and sauna of *Cotton's Health and Fitness Centre* below Cotton's Centre, another giant project from Michael Twigg Brown, completed in 1986 and housing offices of Citicorp and the Canadian Imperial Bank of Commerce.

We live in a narcissistic, pampered age, an age when personal image and physical shape is everything; as you stand on the travelator leading to Price Waterhouse at number one, London Bridge, mirrors galore will tell you everything you desire to know. So much energy and enterprise, such self-esteem, the foreign visitor may exclaim; and still more to come when the next phase of London Bridge City develops (currently there is much empty, cleared land between Hay's and Tower Bridge). Yet, David Kemp's Navigators seems to point to a phoney, almost deranged new world; Allen Jones' painted steel sculpture 'Dancers' in the towering Cotton Centre atrium seems to express an emotional ambivalence: whether to fly or float, be invaded by sunshine, or blackness. It is likely, as always, that the artist will grab the last say.

And so we will stray away from this place with contradictory feelings and thoughts about an era we have just left; oh yes, the tourist of tomorrow will tell you, the British, Thatcherite 1980's when everything was unreal and nothing had substance; a gigantic act of manipulation and image making and a crazied attempt to impose something made up onto a more substantial, more honest past; stumble away across the street, and down Weston Street or Stainer Street tunnels, and back into another century.

TEMPORA · MUTANTUR · NOS · ET · MUTAMUR · IN · ILLIS ·              · ST · OLAVE'S · SOUTHWARK · 1739 · 1928

Above: An engraving by William Washington. Courtesy: Guildhall Library. The demolished church (architect: Henry Flitcroft), dates from 1740 when the old, very ancient church was rebuilt. This print has been reissued by dealers Abbott and Holder. The Builder, 1844 has interior views of the church, before and after the fire; Southwark Local Studies has an impressive framed drawing of the church, by Donald Maxwell, and the demolished church was also depicted by Henry Rushbury. George Washington's engraving is interesting in the way it lessens the brutality of the demolition by highlighting the interior brickwork and the diversity of human activity.

Above: *Battlebridge Lane*; pencil drawing by Alan Stapleton from his book *London Lanes*, Allen Lane, 1930. The street name is a reference to the stream here and its bridge at the time of the abbots of the Abbey of Battle in Sussex who owned the land and had a house here. 1920's photograph of this view in SBR, II.

**Above:** *Tooley Street front of old warehouse premises of distillers Messrs Boord & Co*: on corner of Morgans Lane, the building once stretched down to the riverside. Architect: Aston Webb, 1900. The artist contrasts the imposing building with the fragile looking bare trees.

Opposite: *Detail from the western facade of Denmark House, 15, Tooley Street,* designed by S.D. Adshed in 1908 for the Bennett Steamship Company, and now part of the private London Bridge Hospital, together with the adjoining Emblem House, which has a modern rear; there is a connecting footbridge into the converted Chamberlain's Wharf warehouse behind.

Above: *Shipwrights Arms*, on corner of Bermondsey Street; the brightly painted floral motives continue on both sides of the black painted ground floor: an almost theatrical facade.

Above: *Black and gold mosaic by Colin Gill of St Olave* on the side of the Tooley Street entrance to St Olaf House, designed by H.S. Goodhart-Rendel in 1931 as headquarters of the Hay's Wharf Company, now occupied by actuaries and consultants Bacon & Woodrow. The building contrasts with the adjacent No 1, London Bridge and 1850's Chamberlain's Wharf; it has interesting details: riverside railings, lettering, courtyard entrance ceiling, etc.

Above: *Magistrate's Court, Tooley Street*; built 1904; architect: J.D. Butler (a police station architect who also designed Wapping Police Station). The building has a side entrance in Boss Street. To be contrasted with the much more functional design of Crown Court, built 1979-82, P.S.A. Architects in English Grounds (opposite HMS Belfast). Article on Tower Bridge Stipendiary Magistrate Justin Phillips in Southwark News, January 5th, 1995; and an account of 'a day in the life of Tower Bridge Magistrate's Court' in Southward News, October 10th, 1991.

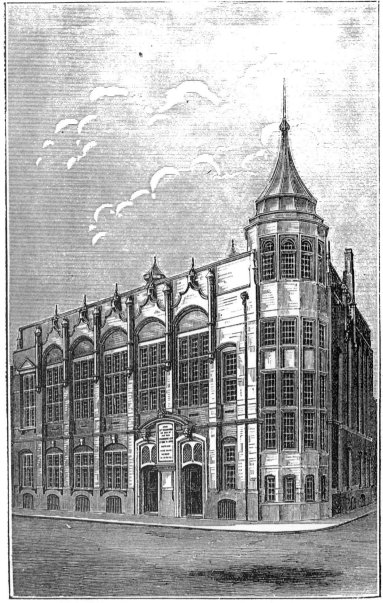

Opposite: *The Public Institute, in Fair Street*; a drawing from Southwark Annual, 1899; architects: Stock, Page and Stock. The building was erected by the Trustees of the United Charities of St Olave and St John, and opened November 28th, 1898 by the Duke of Cambridge. Built on the site of an old non-conformist chapel, later used as an engineering workshop, then as a home of the County of Surrey Temperance Society. Facilities included club rooms, a gymnasium, library and large hall.

Above: *Former offices of the St Olave's Union at 283, Tooley Street*; architects: Newman & Newman; a drawing from the London Argus, September 23rd, 1899; occupied in recent years by London Borough of Southwark Social Services, and now converted into flats as part of Millennium Square. Tower Wharf is a modern development just to the west. Devon Mansions, built in 1888, are opposite.

Above: *South view of Queen Elizabeth's Free Grammar School in Tooley Street.* A drawing by R.B. Schnebbelie, engraved by Wise, published by Robert Wilkinson, 1813 (with map). St Olave's Grammar School was established in 1561 by Queen Elizabeth I, and occupied buildings shown in this attractive print until 1830 when demolished to make way for the new railway. Another building occupied a site in Bermondsey Street until demolished in 1849. The school then moved to the eastern end of Tooley Street; the building standing today was erected 1892-95.

The shot tower in the background was erected in 1808 for manufacturing bullets (molten lead was dropped into water from it). It was destroyed during Topping's wharf fire in 1843, together with St Olave's church (shown in right-hand corner), subsequently rebuilt.

The other grammar school established at the same time was St Saviour's; at London Bridge until 1843 when it moved to Sumner Street: Robert Wilkinson prints of this school were published in 1815. Both schools amalgamated in 1896. There is a history by R.C. Carrington: *Two schools: a history of St Olave's and St Saviour's Grammar School.*

Above: *Old St Olave's and St Saviour's School*, Tooley Street; from Southwark Annual, 1894; built 1892-5, architect: F.W. Mountford (architect of the Old Bailey, Battersea Town Hall, etc); the central frieze shows two schoolboys, one with cricket bat, one with book; this part of the building is a large hall with gallery. The school moved to Orpington in 1968 and Lambeth College now occupies the building. Photograph of the schools' staff, 1936 in SBR, II.

Above: King of Belgium pub, 1897. Tooley Street (corner of Druid Street). Note the ground floor carved pilasters, and the decorative gables.

Above: Bermondsey's first mayor decked out in impressive cloak and regalia; sculpture by Sydney March. A branch of the National Westminster Bank lies in the background.

Above and opposite: *The second St Olave's School*, Bermondsey Street; drawings by T. Allom, engraved by J.H. Kent, from Brayley's History of Surrey.

Below: *The third St Olave's School*, Tooley Street, architect: Allen, Snooke and Stock, replaced by today's building.

# SOUTH OF ST THOMAS STREET: Snowsfields, Weston Street, Melior Street, Crucifix Street, Morocco Street, Leathermarket

SNOWSFIELDS leads out from Newcomen Street, a turning off Borough High Street, into the northern end of Bermondsey Street. It is dominated by an interesting variety of large buildings: at the Bermondsey Street end, numbers one-seven is the large warehouse building of leather firm *S.C. Hall & Son*; opposite is *Olympic Leather Company*, at the top of Hardwidge Street. Some twelve artists and craftspeople work in this street at the *A-Z Studios*. Next comes *Snowsfields Primary School* with entrance in Kirby Grove. We note the elegant plaque recording the enlargement of the school in 1900. This is an impressively large building, and a history of the school by former head teacher Martin Kirby was published recently. In the playground you will find an interesting mural of local scenes, designed and painted by Neil Bunting, Vanessa Johnson and friends in 1987. I spoke to Denise Rogers, current head teacher, and newsletter editor of the Bermondsey Street Association on the telephone in January 1998; she told me of the huge pile of copies of the book waiting to find customers, of her desperate need for more pupils, for more finance.

Opposite the school lies the *Guiness Trust Estate*, now in a truncated version without its original topmost storey as shown in the reproduced photograph. The Guiness Trust was especially active in Southwark: its first 'model dwellings' were opened in 1891 in Brandon Street, Walworth; the Pages Walk site (now replaced by 1976 buildings) in 1895, and the Snowsfields site in 1897. Eleven buildings containing 355 tenements were erected on a site previously covered with a network of courts of small houses.

Opposite lies *Arthur's Mission*, with the commemorating dates 1865-1893 inscribed on the street facade, and two memorial stones dated 1893 commemorating the former superintendent S.R. Pearce and teachers of the old Snowsfields Ragged School. A Pentecostal Gospel Chapel currently uses the building.

Across the Weston Street junction we find a block of almost a century later: *Ronald McDonald House* opened in June 1990, architects: Ansell and Bailey; run by the Evelina Family Trust it provides accommodation for parents of sick children at Guy's Hospital. Evelina Children's Hospital opened in 1869 in Southwark Bridge Road (opposite the Fire Brigade Headquarters). It was financed by Baron Ferdinand de Rothschild in memory of his wife Evelina. In the foyer of the new building we note an interesting semi-abstract wood cut-out panel showing trees with birds.

This building strives to convey a sense of warmth and comfort, which is totally and utterly absent in the adjacent six storey car park. Ugly, Ugly, Ugly! The alienated Londoner will once again scream out. Beyond, at the Kipling Street junction is the large *Miller of Mansfield*, a pub popular with students; and nearby the *Britannia*, and *Guy's Arms*.

Above: *Guiness Trust Buildings*, Snowsfields, 1898; the original structure, as seen from Kirby Grove. A central courtyard lies beyond the colonnaded entrance. Very similar in style to Evelina Mansions, New Church Road, Camberwell.

Opposite: *The Rose pub sign*, on corner of Snowsfields and Weston Street. A large, dramatic sign for a spacious old pub with an open hearth fire, and a variety of pictures, including a figurative mural.

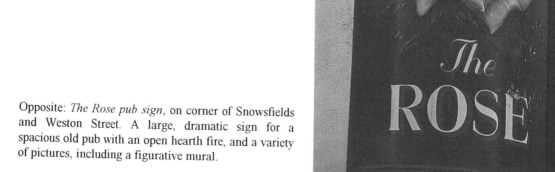

WESTON STREET formerly stretched from Great Dover Street to St Thomas Street. Today housing developments have truncated its southern end, and the street branches out from Wild's Rents, a turning off Long Lane. John Webbe Weston was a local landowner in the early nineteenth century. No tourist will venture down to this bottom end, for sure, yet the twin turrets of Tower Bridge lit up at night-time and viewed down here from the Tabard Gardens housing estate cast enchantment and stimulate the sense that the great world is at our doorstep, although in spirit we may feel far away from it.

Much less off the beaten track is the Leathermarket complex beyond the Long Lane junction. The 1879 old *Leather Exchange* is the architectural centrepiece of this thriving small business complex owned and managed by London Workspace, a division of London Industrial PLC who acquired the buildings in 1993, saving them from demolition when a multi-storey office block was intended. The adjacent *Leathermarket* buildings date from 1833 onwards and are much less ornate. Buildings to the south and north were replaced in the 1960's with the concrete blocks Trowbray House and Lafone House. An illustrated promotional brochure *The Leather Market Review* was published in 1995 and highlights external and internal architectural features. Access to the Leathermarket is via the Leathermarket Street reception and cafe area, and through two arches in Weston Street. Looking at the long lists of businesses in each unit, one's response must be initially of bafflement: what do all these people actually do? If you check the telephone directory some basic information may be found for some, others may not be listed, but the overall impression is of a hive of creativity-based enterprises: there are theatre companies, for instance, and the service organisation the *Independent Theatre Council* is here; there are designers and architects, artists and model makers; wine merchants: *Morris and Verdin* at unit 10, *Cave Cru Classe* at unit 13; coloured paper specialists *G.F. Smith* are at units 1/2, and *H. Page Engineering Services* at unit 15. Moving into a more rarefied realm: 'Two worlds' is a monthly spiritualist magazine, established in 1887, published today at unit 7. Above is the *London Glassblowing Workshop and Gallery*, Peter Layton's successful and internationally recognised enterprise which moved here from Rotherhithe in 1995. His achievement is surveyed in a booklet catalogue *Twenty-one today*: an exhibition celebrating twenty-one years, and twenty-one glassmakers associated with the London Glass Blowing Workshop, 1976-1997; and he himself is the author of an important international survey *Glass art*, published by A & C Black.

Progressing northwards, at number 106, on the corner of Leathermarket Street in a building dated 1930 you find the head office of a housing trust *Open Door*; they specialise in housing for disadvantaged people (with mental health, drink and drug problems). Beyond the Bermondsey Village Hall (used for many community activities), at the southern end of Kirby Grove we find a new housing block at number 80: *Bridgewalk Heights*, with red balconies and a basement-level car park (cars are much more visible here than people). More businesses are located at the northern end of Weston Street; opposite number 70, a disused warehouse, there is a small business 'enclave' at numbers 75-83; at number 75: *S.N. Bartarya & Co*, accountants; at number 77: *PRW Design Partnership*; and *Calvert Jackson Nokes*, solicitors, for example – strange names! The old *Rose pub* is on the corner of Snowfields opposite a green domed block, with flats above, and shops below. *Tower Satay*, Malaysian, Indonesian and Indian restaurant is at number 62; at number 60, Isambard House (with attractive wrought iron gate), offices of *West & Partners*, planning consultants.

Michael West and his partner Chris Francis are former Southwark Council planners; their previous office was on the sixth floor of Battlebridge House, Tooley Street, now demolished. *Barnardo's*, the charity, have a London project office at numbers 52-58, providing services for homeless families and refugees. *Merlin's* at number 48, with its eye-catching external mural describes itself as an 'olde English restaurant'. Next door, across Melior Place, is a jarring, ugly block Capital House. Across the road is the *Greenwood Theatre/London Bridge Studios*, built in 1975 by the trustees of Guy's Hospital, through the generosity of Sir James Mantle Greenwood, a hospital governor 1960-1969, a long brown brick facade with narrow windows.

Above: *Warehouses, Weston Street*; from the Builder, 1876; architects: Newman and Billing. Premises of leather firm Cleeve & Hooper.

Above: *Mural by Jonathan Huxley overlooking playground at Leathermarket Gardens*. Blue, green and red shapes on a yellow background.

MELIOR STREET is dominated by the *Roman Catholic Church Our Lady of La Salette and St Joseph*. The church exterior communicates mystery, withdrawal and unworldliness, the hospital blocks towering behind (Thomas Guy House, 1996, stamped all over with the Guy's coat of arms, with thrusting cornices, and blue window frames; and Wolfson House, 1977, with windows like long strips of bandaging) a brutal matter of factness. I have often passed through here, and not finding the church in Pevsner, I telephoned Father Cooley for factual information. The church began, he told me, in nearby Webb Street in 1848 in a disused medical school building. Today's building dates from 1861, architect: Edmund J. Kelly, the parish houses next door from 1868, and the parish hall from the 1930's.

The *City Banking College*, with a large forecourt, occupies the old school premises which reached their present-day form in the 1890's. The school moved out in 1978 to a new site in Little Dorrit Court, off Borough High Street. SBR, II has a photograph of a class of happy school boys in 1932. The City Banking College is a private establishment set by Kadz Kahn from Guyana., but is also a 'resource centre' for management courses at the University of Leicester and also works in collaboration with the Institute of Bankers and the Guildhall University. Financial Training PLC also run accountancy courses here. The college attracts many students from West Africa, the administrator informed me.

The *Manna Centre* occupies the 1950's nursery part of the old school; set up by Nannette Ffrench and Raymond Towey in 1983, and, inevitably, precariously funded, it provides help and services to the needy, hungry, and homeless. A leaflet account of the organisation and its development concludes with some heartening words:
'Most important of all is the atmosphere of peace and friendship which the Centre promotes; we have an open door policy and everyone is accepted as they are – with their own gifts, stories, and problems just like all of us. We try to help them become more fully aware of their own worth and potential.'

In MELIOR PLACE adjacent to the Manna Day Centre we find the *Glass House*: the residence of a pop star one might imagine at first; the sculptor and artist Andrew Logan has his studio here, and the house is owned by Michael Davis, who converted a car repair garage adding a new floor and a glass roof in 1990. Michael Davis worked as a designer for some 25 years. Currently he is Chairman of the Bermondsey Street Association, project director of the Zandra Rhodes Foundation Museum of Fashion and Textiles and Chairman of the trustees of the Andrew Logan Museum of Sculpture in Berriew, Montgomeryshire. In 1997 during the Open House weekend some 875 visitors were admitted to this Bermondsey fantasy place, he told me.

Later I learnt that Peter Logan, the brother, designed the wind sculpture in Old Kent Road, outside the Tesco store.

Opposite: *the Horseshoe inn*, 1897, at the bottom of Melior Street; an intimate pub with attractive iron railings, in a dramatic setting. Article in Southwark Pub Guide Series in South London Press, April 3rd, 1998.

FENNING STREET is a turning off Melior Street. Here you will find the premises of *Daxbourne Ltd*, 'the UK's leading distributor of wigs and hairpieces'. ST THOMAS STREET runs next to the railway viaduct and here as elsewhere you will find a variety of businesses occupying the arches: at number 61: *French, Flint and Ormco Ltd*, dealers in glass bottles, jars and plastic containers; at number 73: *Smithfield Office Furniture*; at numbers 77-79 a printer the *Woodrow Press*. By way of contrast at *Beckett House* opposite you find the offices of the HM Immigration Service.

St Thomas Street continues at its eastern end as CRUCIFIX LANE. The holy rood or cross of Bermondsey was a Saxon cross found in the Thames in 1117; believed to have miraculous powers it was an object of pilgrimage in the abbey until the dissolution when it was set up on Horsleydown Common, at the eastern end of what is now Crucifix Lane until destroyed in 1559. At one end of the lane is *Chapter House*, a currently empty, and ugly modern office block; close by are the boarded premises of Ash and Ash; at the other end the immeasurably more attractive Globe House, with redevelopment planned. In between you find the *Horns* public house, *Crown Security*, former premises of wine merchants John Egan and Son (established in 1860) and the refurbished five-storey block now occupied by environmental management consultants *Aspinwall & Co*. Opposite at number 11 under the railway arches is *Classic Porsche and Restoration*. Again, a strange, but not untypical mixture.

Above: *Rear view of the premises at numbers 44, 43, 42 and 41, Crucifix Lane*; drawing, 1876, by J.P. Emslie. Courtesy: Southwark Local Studies Library.

When buildings change their use, when new people move into an area and stamp their new identity on a place there is a sense of incongruity, a feeling that things are not quite right. You have this impression in the turnings opposite Tanner Street: MOROCCO STREET (formerly Upper Russell Street) branching off to the left and leading into LEATHERMARKET STREET (formerly known simply as Market Street – leading into Manning Street).

*Engineering Design Consultants* have their offices at number 106, Bermondsey Street in an old Midland Bank. Just around the corner at 1a, Morocco Street, lights burn late at night in the offices of *Dransfield Design* (Jonathan Dransfield and Ruth Owens). Their partnership is of special importance to the locality: they have been responsible for new developments such as the Morocco Store, and the adjacent new block, new residential buildings at number 105, Bermondsey Street, and on the old Sarson's site at the corner of Tower Bridge Road. At number 3, Morocco Street you find office of *Curtis Hoy*, a marketing and sales promotion agency for drinks, cosmetics, and computer games companies; also here is *Octavo*, a design company; at number five, premises of *Mandene*, flooring contractors set up by Alan Rackham some twenty-five years ago; and at number nine *Planart Reproduction*, plate-makers and printers. Opposite lie very expensive flats, the Morocco side of Leathermarket Court.

The circular corner towers of numbers one, two-four, Leathermarket Street are special features. At number two there are offices of *Alandene and Stavedene* (a related interior design firm), at number four offices of *Anthony Bowhill* who specialise in planning permission, and planning appeal work nationally. Mr Bowhill has been in private practice for many years; he set up in 1984 in Lavington Street, then in Southwark Street in 1986 and moving to Leathermarket Street in 1988. The *Morocco Store* has been so named by the developers and is advertised loud and clear as such. Andrew Wadsworth's Landworth Properties company issue a prestige brochure for this new development. It contains architectural drawings by Hanley Calvert, an aerial photograph, and a 1940's photograph of the building when known as Swan House, built 1852, when a warehouse for Scottish Malt Products. *Architype*, architects occupy ground floor premises.

At the lower end of Leathermarket Street, at numbers 20/22, *Richard Scales* has been operating his bookbinding business (established in 1975) for some ten years. Much of his firm's activity is general trade work rather than the 'up-market' specialities of SSZ he told me. At number 26 there is the newly built *Leathermarket Neighbourhood Housing Office*. A small archway leads into a children's playground behind. To the west (on the wall of number 106, Weston Street) we discover to our considerable delight, a small, colourful, happy mural by *Jonathan Huxley*, an initiative of the Bermondsey Street Association. (Article in the Guardian, March 1st, 1993).

TYERS GATE runs parallel to Leathermarket Street. The old leather warehouses have now been converted and are used for mixed residential and business purposes. Estate agents *Daniel Cobb* opened recently on the ground floor of number two, and nearby in Bermondsey Street, next to the World Miracle Outreach organisation is another new firm *Williams Lynch Ltd*, residential sales and lettings. There are studios at number seven, Tyers Gate.

Above: *The Bermondsey Leather and skin market*: the arcaded area which stood at the eastern end of the site.

Above: *The London Leather Exchange*; from the Builder, 1879; architects: George Elkington. Ceased functioning as a centre for buying and selling about 1912. Currently awaits new tenants. This elaborate, decorative facade contrasts with the dull tower blocks across the road marked by a complete lack of decoration. The turret and clockface have gone, likewise the block to the left, replaced by Lafone House.

# BERMONDSEY'S LEATHER TRADE COMMEMORATED IN ART

Above: *Tanners Arms pub sign*; formerly at 60, Willow Walk, and known as the Willows; closed in 1996 and was boarded up; later, an arson attack in 1997 (Southwark News, February 13th, 1997).

Above: *Old Leather Exchange pub, 15 Leathermarket Street*; based on the relief carved roundel on the exchange building. Pub renamed the Juggler's Arms in 1992.

Above: *Simon the Tanner pub sign*, 321 Long Lane; replaced with new sign early 1990's.

*Relief sculptures on wall of the old Leather Exchange*:
fellmongering, tanning, dressing, weighing/recording,
inspecting/stacking.

# BUTLERS WHARF/SHAD THAMES: Food and Art Emporium

"The buildings are beautiful, but where are the people?" asked the Southwark and Bermondsey News on October 24th, 1991. Today, six years on, there is much more activity here, more people work here, have apartments here, come to eat here, visit the art galleries and museums, but there is still a chilling, clinical coldness to the place, a feeling which sends you scurrying back to a friendlier and warmer place such as your own home. This area's development in the second half of the 1980's emanates from the policies of the LDDC, and of key personalities such as Terence Conran (responsible for the Butlers Wharf block, the Design Museum, restaurants, and the chef school); and Andrew Wadsworth (Jacob's Island Company responsible for New concordia Wharf, China Wharf, and the Circle). Contrasting all this with the view out onto Decima Street, not that far away, one must only conclude that we are in a place conceived and marketed as part of a city of international prestige and power. This is the mood we get from the converted *Butlers Wharf* warehouse (built 1873, architects: Tolley and Dale), with ground floor restaurants and shops and 86 apartments above; and next to it the former *Anchor Brewhouse* (rebuilt 1893-5 by Inskip and McKenzie), converted into offices and 62 flats by Pollard, Thomas and Edwards. Both blocks glare at us haughtily as we cross over Tower Bridge. 'Hong Kong businessman pays £1.5 million for Boilerhouse penthouse' says Dockland News, October 1997; and for that he got: three bedrooms with bathrooms, a private lift, a swimming pool and sauna, marble flooring, a custom-made Italian kitchen.

Starting afresh, creating a new kind of place, creating a new chapter in the history of a great city may well call for an aggressive obliteration of the past: and so we have the sanitising whiteness of the Design Museum, the brilliant blue of the courtyard walls of the Circle, the bright orange of Tower Bridge Piazza.

Amidst so much change, at a time of startling transformation, it is inevitable that people will suffer: Anthony Donaldson's nude fountain figures are just holding on to the central drum structure with their thin arms, are just keeping their heads above water, their possessions (camera, paint box, mouth organ, note book and pen, reading books) seem of scant significance in the frantic effort of survival. We observe with sympathetic curiosity Eduardo Paolozzi's bronze head called 'Newton after James Watts' lying outside the Design Museum, and understand only too well the weary, work-loaded resignation of Shirley Pace's dray horse sculpture at the centre of the Circle.

It seems likely that the artist has the last say, as so often; indeed art galleries have been here since the early 1990's. Some galleries have come and then gone, moving elsewhere: Purdy Hicks (Jayne Purdy and Rebecca Hicks) was at Jacob Street Film Studios, Mill Street, and now is in Hopton Street, Bankside; The Raw Gallery, run by Haydn Reynolds was at the Cooperage, in Gainsford Street for three years and has now moved to the U.S.A. (see article in Southwark News, November 28th, 1996). The site has been taken by another gallery, the Azerbajan Art Center. Reed's Wharf Gallery, run by Stephen Lacey (cousin of architect Nicholas Lacey) has gone to Clerkenwell (article in Southwark News, June 26th, 1997). L'Art Abstrait, formerly in Queen Elizabeth Street, is now run by its lawyer owner David Raybold from his Dulwich home, plus sales through art fairs.

Artistic creativity is invariably unpredictable. No gallery owner, no critic can ever really be sure of what is going to materialise next, so every educated person should pay regular visits to his local galleries where the desire for the excitement of discovery will often be fulfilled. The *Plateau Gallery* opened in 1997 in Brewery Square and shows furniture, glass, metalwork and jewellery. The owner Leo Duval was born in Cyprus and came to London in 1985 graduating in furniture design from Middlesex Polytechnic in 1991. His awareness of quality and informed interest in the applied arts, range of contacts, and tactful courtesy seem the exact requirements for a successful art business. His gallery is spacious with glass walls on three sides and you enter it through the passage way between the two squares, to the south of Copper Row. Graham Coombs-Hoar (*Coombs Contemporary Art*) has been in the art world for many years. He started his own gallery in Folkestone in 1989 and has been at Tower Bridge Piazza since 1994. Much of the work he shows is figurative: the work of Dick French, the dramatic portraits by Limehouse-based artist Stephen Harwood, for example; but not exclusively so: the semi-abstract works by David Greenham inspired by his Isle of Lewis (Outer Hebrides) locality are also stocked. The *Cinegrafix Gallery* also in the square specialises in old cinema posters. Across the square is the *Gallery Differentiate*, 45 Shad Thames, run by Tracey Colman. You will find abstract work here, and the gallery specialises in the steel mesh human form sculpture of David Begbie. Next door at number 43, and inhabiting a somewhat more practical world is *Hideall*, specialising in hand-crafted leather goods and outdoor clothing, run by Michael and Pauline Gebbett (with another shop at Greenwich Market).

Opposite: *Anthony Donaldson's Waterfall* in Tower Bridge Piazza. See chapter for commentary.

The redevelopment of the area south of Butlers Wharf was the work of architects Wickham and Associates for the Berkeley House Docklands Development Ltd, and was completed in 1990: shops at ground floor level, offices and flats above. The three photographs show views interesting for their 'juxtapositions'.

Above: *Brewery Square*, north of Gainsford Street; Torso sculpture by Anthony Donaldson. This view is from Horsleydown Lane.

Opposite: Turreted residences peer down apprehensively onto John Courage's first pub. He established a small brewhouse in 1787 on the site of today's converted Anchor Brewhouse. The view is the south western corner of Tower Bridge Piazza from Horsleydown Lane.

Photography is the speciality of the *Tom Blau Gallery* in Queen Elizabeth Street. It is based at the premises of the Camera Press, international photographic agency, founded by Tom Blau in 1947 and consisting today of some 12 million pictures. A 50 year celebratory show of the agency was held at the gallery in November 1997. For contemporary sculpture you have the *McHardy Sculpture Company*, run by Max and Joanne McHardy in the Cardamon Building, Shad Thames (featured in Docklands News, October 1995). Its promotional leaflet lists some 30 featured artists, established and new, and offers works suitable for many different environments. In recent months I have enjoyed the resin-laminated paper sculptures by Terence Wall, and the enigmatic, sculptured heads by Patricia Volk. In January 1998 I was stuck by a bronze (costing £2400) by Tim Pomeroy called 'Ship of fools' at the entrance and the steel and glazed clay masks by Alasdair Neil MacDonnell. Ian McClure caters for even more eccentric tastes at his shop called *Thesaurus*. He is a trained architect and interior designer from the USA and his shop bulges with textiles, ethnographic art, fossils and minerals, antiques and industrial furniture. 'It's a variety of whimsical objects which seem to work together', he told the South London Press featuring his business in their Focus on a Firm series, September 12th, 1997. *Stitches and Daughters*, at 36 Horsleydown Lane (with another shop in Greenwich) is another unusual speciality shop with an eclectic range of goods aimed at the design-conscious, sophisticated young woman of today.

Close by is the *Riverside Bookshop*, Sylvie Ridgewell's second shop in the area; its corner site is well chosen, and there is a large upmarket general book stock of recent and newly published books, including a good local interest section.

So much then for art, and objets d'art; if all else fails, there is food: some comfort can be had from the many kinds of food on offer, so carefully manufactured and packaged to give us pleasure and to get us back for more. Everyone is aware of the explosion of bars and eating out places over the last ten yeas or so. Feeling pampered, being waited on, indulging in luxury, feeling both within society whilst keeping one's distance from it are perhaps some of the characteristics of this end of the century gastronomic indulgence...and so on to *Mr Conran's Butlers Wharf 'Gastrodrome'*. You can read up the chef's recipes in the Gastrodrome Cookbook, by Rory Ross, published by Pavilion in 1995, and get background information on all the Conran establishments in London and overseas in a small address book directory with postage stamp sized illustrations by Flo Bayley available from the press office at the Clove Building. The *Pont de la tour* was opened in September 1991; caricatures by Sem depicting early twentieth century Parisian cafe society line the south wall; the menu is strongly influenced by regional French and Italian cooking. The complex also includes the food store, the bakery, (some 50 different breads are baked daily), and the wine merchant (over 600 different wines from around the world), all of which are open to the public. The head chef is David Burke. The *Blue Print Cafe* at the Design Museum opened in 1989; the head chef here is Jeremy Lee. The *Cantina del Ponta* at the riverside nearby opened in 1992 and is Mediterranean in flavour. The mural by New Zealand artist Timna Wollard is especially striking: full of carefully painted figures, it depicts the traffic of food from barges to market stalls, to kitchens and chefs, with a wine cellar to conclude. You can also see a wooden model of Tower Bridge. The head chef here is Jonathan Nicholson. *Butlers Wharf Chop House* opened in 1993, head chef Andrew Johns. The preparation of food is given a theatrical quality here in Shad Thames: as we pass through we are encouraged to enjoy the chefs at their work through open glass windows: a simple, yet wonderful stroke of imagination in this sombre old place.

Other food places are here too. Mr Conran has not been allowed to gain a monopoly: a new Indian restaurant the *Bengal Clipper* is in the Cardamon Building, Shad Thames, the walls decorated with attractive modern classical Indian art; the *Hing Lee Chinese Restaurant* is at 32, Curlew Street, on the corner of Gainsford Street. *Captain Tony's Pizza Parlour* is at 41, Lafone Street. There are more informal places too: the *Bespoke Sandwich Company* in the Piazza; *Schullers Sandwich Bar* at 47, Shad Thames; the tiny *Al Roubna* in the Circle; pubs include the *Anchor Tap* in Horsleydown Lane, and the *Swift and Stump* in Gainsford Street. There are food stores too: *Essentials and Lots More* in the Piazza and the *Circle Store* at the Shad Thames end of Queen Elizabeth Street.

Food and drink are also subjects of vocational and academic study here too. The *Butlers Wharf Chef School* opened recently in Shad Thames in an attempt to deal with shortages of skilled chefs and front-of-house personnel. You can see the training in progress as you pass by, or test the skills being trained at the *Apprentice* restaurant on the site. Edward Bramah's *Tea and Coffee Museum* (shortly to move into the Tamarind Building, Maguire Street) is the first of its kind and has a very successful, eventful six years since opening in 1992 (see Southwark and Bermondsey News, February 27th, 1992): coffee grinders, teapots galore, equipment, paintings and prints have been lovingly collected by this expert in the tea and coffee trades. Quiller Press has published his exhaustive survey of novelty teapots and will also publish his work on the British tea trade. An introductory guide to the museum is available, and income is also derived from the tea and coffee room, and the retail shop which will stock an extensive range of books. Mr Bramah is confident of an ever-increasing number of visitors and predicts 40,000 for 1998.

Above: Part of the *Circle*, Queen Elizabeth Street, 1990, architect: CZWG. The bright blue tiles and cut-out shapes create a dramatic effect. Nick Campbell, Roger Zogolovitch (no longer a partner), Rex Wilkinson and Piers Gough trained together at the Architectural Association in the late 1960's. The firm is especially active in the field of private housing in London: within the docklands area you can enjoy: Cascades, E14, 1988; China Wharf, SE1, 1988; Wolfe Crescent, SE16, 1989; Basque Court, SE16, 1993; The Mission, E14 (conversion), 1994; Bow Quarter, E3, 1995; Dundee Wharf, E14, 1997. Works in progress include: Bankside Lofts, SE1; Batson's and Regent's Wharfs, E14; Atlas Wharf, E14; Tunnel Wharf, SE16; Mile End Park.

Piers Gough, and his exciting original creations, is discussed in two recent articles in Harpers & Queens, November 1995; and Perspectives, December/January 1997.

Opposite: *Jacob, the Circle dray horse*; sculpted by Chichester based equestrian sculptor Shirley Pace. The Times, October 2nd, 1987 shows the horse being lowered into place from a helicopter. The work was commissioned by Jacobs Island Company to commemorate the brewery stables formerly on the site, as well as the countless dray horses of assorted ancestry who had worked in Bermondsey. The artist comments: 'My objective was to portray the dignified tolerance and the power of these horses plus the hint of resignation to man's direction and the vagaries of a cold wet windy winter...'

# QUEEN ELIZABETH, GAINSFORD, CURLEW, LAFONE STREETS

QUEEN ELIZABETH STREET is the southern most part of the Butlers Wharf redevelopment area, the first street we encounter when coming from Bermondsey; with the melodramatic *Circle* as its climax near the Shad Thames junction, it is a startling street to encounter and one to take our visitors down. When we reach the central theatrical arena we find four blocks with zigzagging little windows and a central line of balconies. The balconies continue zigzagging down the street beyond: a veritable forest of balconies with wooden supports: an architect's hearty reply to all those timid, fake balconies we encounter so often in docklands. There are entrance foyers on both sides of the Circle: the heads of the security guards can be glimpsed within, sitting at equally monstrous desks, with bizarre lamps and green background walls.

The approach to the Circle takes us past: to the right, *Boss House* (two large residential blocks with a dramatic glass lift structure adjoining the two), and extending down to Tooley Street; then *Raven Wharf*, currently under construction, then *Albion House*, headquarters of Blue Star and other shipping companies; to the left: *Queen Elizabeth the Queen Mother House* (SSAFA Forces Help), then the *Camera Press* building (an important, famous photographic agency), architects: Panter Hudsmith, a converted 1960's warehouse block, with two corner balconies and unusual timber panels on the upper two storeys, then the *Flag Store* block, and *Jubilee Yard* behind, followed by *Sandpiper House*. The *Circle Restaurant* is on the corner of Curlew Street; beyond, to the left *Sputnik Travel*, the *Flower Wharf Shop, Sarkpoint Reprographics, Bourdillon Stationery and Business Services*, a dry cleaners, and finally the *Circle Store*; at last, you might gasp: a place at which to buy a sustaining bag of nuts! Opposite the Circle Restaurant is a tiny sandwich bar *Al Loubna*. Within the Circle, and overlooking the garden courtyard area: architects *Haeger, Lindsey and Wilkins* (unit 4), *Contact Securities Ltd* (unit 8), *The Amos Partnership*, architects and designers (unit 9), *ISS Cleaning* firm (unit 10), *Equator International*, marketing (unit 12), and *Facilities Company* (unit 12a), providing company hospitality, parties, etc, established in 1988.

Beyond the Circle there is the air travel office *Stars and Stripes*, and finally the *Circle sales and letting office*. *Number three, Millennium Square* comes as a surprise: a wholly different kind of block, which creates a pleasing effect with its purple columns, green balconies and piled up angled windows.

GAINSFORD STREET is equally startling, if less dramatic, and it too can be perambulated with interest. At the western end, there are the high-powered offices of *Clutton's*, and on the other side of the entrance to Brewery Square, *Guiness Flight Hambro Asset Management Ltd*; the Cooperage, with its columned portico, has an almost aggressively intrusive presence, out of harmony with the small terrace opposite. It was part of the Anchor Brewery complex and was converted by Wickham Associates; there are flats above, a gallery at number 7, the entrance to the Crown Prosecution Service at number 8, and *Finlayson Design* at number 9. This is a street which our politicians of the future will remember in years to come: the *London School of Economics hall of residence*, Conran Roche architects, 1989 is here: six-storeyed, with student rooms grouped into flats, with balconies. No doubt most students here, as elsewhere, accept what they have put onto their plates. Opposite is number 54, called *Thames Heights*; number 57 next door has a central blue section, contrasting with the cream brickwork, and with the mock loading bays on either side. *Nutmeg House*, at number 60, Conran Roche again, is a working environment: even on Sundays the architects at *Savil, Peach and Gence* on the ground floor are hard at work, with models, plans and journals all over tables. Also here are: *Kingsway Advertising, Safety Assessment Federation Ltd*, the *Association of Business Sponsorship of the Arts* (ABSA), and disability organisations: the *Centre for Accessible Environments*, the *Employers Forum on Disability*, and the *Prince of Wales Advisory Group on Disability*.

Beyond the Curlew Street junction, we find still further new blocks planned: Galliard Homes and Frogmore Estates announce their plans for new, desirable residences: *Millennium View, The White House*, and *Old Bell Gate*. Opposite is the *Butlers Wharf Business Centre* (described in the Curlew Street section), and beyond the *Coriander Building*, on the corner of Maguire Street. This is a sensitive and pleasing conversion of two Victorian warehouses into modern offices, with a staircase in between. Here we might observe on week days the egg-headed whiz kids bouncing to and from their offices: *H & E Johnson*, chartered accountants, *Mercury Design, IQ group of companies, Digital Mail Ltd, R.H. Wrightson & Associates* (economic consultants), and the *Ignition Marketing Group*.

An empty old warehouse currently stands behind the LSE Hall of Residence - weed infested, windows broken, stonework crumbling, it enables further appreciation of sensitive restoration and conversion.

The old spice works (Butlers Wharf Company) opposite the Coriander Buildings have now gone, replaced by a car park (profile article in Southwark News, March 27th, 1997).

Above: *Queen's Court, Queen Street* (today's Lafone Street); drawing, 1886, by J.P. Emslie. Courtesy: Southwark Local Studies Library.

CURLEW STREET runs from Queen Elizabeth Street into the eastern stretch of Shad Thames. We note, as we scurry along, the attractive nineteenth century residential terrace at numbers 24-28.

Beyond lies a new warehouse conversion: Tamarind Court, extending into Maguire Street. Opposite, to the west, a wide, open space with two wall facades at either end, leaving future developments to the imagination of the observer. The *Butlers Wharf Business Centre* which opened in 1986 is to the right, with another entrance in Gainsford Street. I made a list of all the businesses there in late January 1998 to compare with one published in Southwark and Bermondsey News, October 24th, 1991. Not inevitably, only one name remains: management consultants Terence J. Cocks & Associates. For the record, here is a list of today's tenants:

Ground floor: *HAC Printers; Jumbleys Cafe; Thames Communications*(repairs fax machines); *Centre management*.

Second floor: *Seafarer Cruising; Equisys Ltd* (computer software); *EML Ltd; CNS Ltd* (telecommunications, maintenance and consultancy).

Third floor: *Gracia Abreu Design; Harland Design; Jonathan Miller design consultants; Hawkeye Securities*.

Fourth floor: *Career Concepts; Academy Flooring Services; T.J. Cocks & Associates; Privatisation International; Blackman Productions; Cornerstone; Paracetamol Information Centre; Brandon Harris Co.* (public relations); *Segal Recruitment*.

Fifth floor: *Reynolds Bradshaw* (tax consultants); *Compuquest; SBP Ltd* (printers).

Curlews in Curlew Street?, you might wonder. The street name derives apparently from a miller John Curlew who rented the nearby mill at St Saviour's Dock in 1536.

LAFONE STREET commemorates an individual too: Alfred Lafone, MP for Bermondsey 1886-92, and 1895-1900. With Henry Lafone he was also a director of leather factors Boutcher, Mortimore & Co. On the western side, just off Shad Thames, large unit number signs hang. Many of the units are still unlet, but here amidst hard businesses such as *Houlder*, off-shore engineers, and *J.F. Chowd & Co*, tax consultants, you find *Man and Boy hairdressers*, at unit 57, and *Captain Tony's Pizza Parlour* at unit 41, set up in 1991 and 1992 respectively.

# AROUND ST SAVIOUR'S DOCK:
## Shad Thames, Maguire Street, Mill Street

St Saviour's Dock is framed to the west by the lower reach of Shad Thames, round into Maguire Street, and to the east by Mill Street. Warehouse blocks, now all residential in SHAD THAMES have their names preserved in large letters: Jamaica Wharf, Dockhead Wharf, Shuters Wharf, Christian's Wharf, St George's Wharf, St Saviour's Wharf, St Andrew's Wharf, and Java Wharf; now all painted up with little balconies added: reds, blues and greens strive to bring life into this sombre region. All this contrasts with *Saffron Wharf* at number 18, Conran Roche building of 1990, currently being marketed as a block of thirteen apartments, and the Conran shop contracts building at number 22, 1990, architect: Michael Hopkins. This was originally the *David Mellor Building*, with ground floor shop for sale of kitchen equipment, but the firm (which specialises in the design and manufacture of cutlery) moved out after only a few years. Whiteness, greyness, much glass, and a total absence of decoration, no-nonsense, individuality extinguished: the sanitising modernist style. Four thin columns at ground level rise through the upper storeys of the building with balconies at the top. CD Partnership has offices here - and is the design section of the Conran organisation. *Cinnamon Wharf* is a seven storey warehouse conversion of 1986 and has a dingy anonymity. The derelict block next to it, with 'Butlers Wharf Ltd' spelt out on the red brickwork is a delight and worth seeing in its current state. No doubt the sanitising buckets will descend here soon.

Around the corner in MAGUIRE STREET you will find the Design Museum, and the Clove Building. The *Design Museum* is a converted 1950's warehouse, two storeys knocked into one, and a new floor built on the roof, terraces facing the river, the first floor one housing the Blueprint Cafe. Shad Thames runs under this structure which, when first encountered, seems baffling rather than ugly or beautiful. It was opened by Mrs Thatcher on July 5th, 1989. At the entrance a board records innumerable institutions, charitable bodies and businesses which have given financial assistance, including overseas embassies; an adjacent plaque records Lord Reilly, 1912-90, chairman of the museum, and director of the Design Council 1960-77. When I was there in March 1998 the exhibition then was the Conran Foundation collection, 1997. Forthcoming exhibitions were announced featuring Ferdinand Porsche, Bosch (famous for its washing machines), Charles and Ray Eames and David Mellor. I spent an hour or so in the shop; gazed in through glass cases at clocks and watches, mugs and pens, urban masks, telephones, cork screws, key rings and cufflinks. There are bookshelves selling us specialist publications, with an emphasis on architecture of today, specialist monographs from Phaidon (there is a large series on specific buildings), beautiful surveys from the German Taschen Verlag, and the pocket book series from Ellipsis (and German partners Könemann), taking us round contemporary architecture in cities and countries throughout the world (some 17 titles in print, and at least eight more planned). The absurdity of the London fixation then hit me hard. The new *Waterfront: a world-wide urban success story*, by American Ann Breen and Dick Rigby from Thames & Hudson also grabbed my attention. The *Clove Building* next door is a 1989 conversion of a 1930's warehouse, architects: Allies and Morrison. It houses an office furniture firm Bulo, and the Coffee and Tea Museum next door. The London County Council *Shad Thames Pumping Station* with wide arched windows and terracotta glazed brickwork dates from 1906-8, and the warehouse on the corner of Shad Thames from about 1820, to form the new *Spice Quay* development. Ever curious about street names, I checked Sheila Fairfield's book, and there she suggests that Maguire is probably Rev. Dr. Robert Maguire, 1826-90, rector of St Olave's from 1875.

MILL STREET is just off the tourist beaten track, yet it is an interesting street, with considerable drama. The new block on the Jamaica Road corner *Scott's Sufferance Wharf* seems to be battling it out with Holy Trinity Church for supremacy here. On the ground floor you find an estate agents *Spring*, the *Laundry Box*, dry cleaning business, *Ebsco Subscription Services*, computer firm *New Leaf Ltd*. Opposite, Tower Bridge Buildings has long balconies, and a curious little arched entrance. At Lloyds Wharf you find maritime companies such as *TMC Marine Consultants*, and *Ferryman, Fyand and Hudson*, consulting marine surveyors. Opposite at Mill House/Little Britain there are two eateries: the *Mill Street Cafe*, and *La Lanterna Pizzeria*; an Italian restaurant *Tentazioni*, a long dining room with orange walls is across the road. There are more businesses in Unity Wharf, with a side passage and decorative twisting iron gateways: including *Griffin Interior Construction* and chartered building surveyors and property consultants *Richard Hartley Partnership*. Then comes the first big dramatic encounter: *Vogan's Mill* is totally unexpected; we twist our necks gawping at the tall tower, expecting to glimpse the rich and famous descending the prestigious staircase into the film-set style foyer with its brown pillars and yellow walls, fully visible at street level. Opposite Vogan's Mill, on the corner of Jacob Street, is a new block *Hobbs Court*. Here you will find the offices of *John D. Wood*, lettings and management firm established in 1872 with some eleven offices throughout London and Surrey; also here are architects *Sampson & Associates*, established in 1984, who specialise in the design of pubs, clubs and restaurants. After St Saviour's Wharf we encounter the next dramatic discovery of the street: *New Concordia Wharf*, the earliest and most significant warehouse conversion: built originally in 1885 and consisting of warehouses, mill with water tower and courtyard, the property was acquired by Andrew Wadsworth in 1980 and converted with meticulous care by Pollard Thomas and Edwards. A prestigious brochure from the Jacobs Island Company has two architectural elevation drawings of the site. A chimney juts out into the street and we enter the courtyard through painted gates. At ground floor level there are offices and a swimming pool to the right. You find *BUJ Architects* here (and also on the ground floor of China Wharf); *SMi* are conference organisers. *Kirker Europe* run exclusive short break holidays; *H & P Design Associates* have an extensive office here, *IKOS* is a fund management company and a securities broking house; *John Liddall & Son* are stockbrokers and *Rudston Products* are raw skin brokers. New Concordia Wharf adjoins *China Wharf*, another dramatic creation from CZWG and Andrew Wadsworth; built in 1988 with striking riverside red 'cut-out' design framing doors and windows with balconies, and 'scalloped' white and pink rear wall.

Above: *St Saviour's Dock*; a nineteenth century 'reconstruction' drawing by Jen Parker, 1997. New Concordia Wharf (named after Concordia, near Kansas City, Missouri, USA, source for much imported grain), built in 1885, is shown on the left.

A passage way to the left of the building leads to Nicholas Lacey's sparkling new footbridge across the dock. After the elephantine quality of much that we have seen in Mill Street it has an almost balletic lightness of touch; it is used on the cover of the LDDC Bermondsey riverside booklet. The practice, established in 1971, with its offices nearby in Reed's Wharf, is especially well-known for the Crown Reach development at Millbank, and on the Isle of Dogs Herons Quay, and the Advanced Textile Products warehouse and factory. The firm also designed the footbridge at Rotherhithe Tunnel, Limehouse end, and is currently working on a new arts centre for Urban Space Holdings at Trinity Buoy Wharf.

Out in the river lies the *Harpy*, headquarters of Andrew Wadsworth's property company. Between 1905 and 1979 it was sited opposite HMS Belfast in front of Customs House, and used by customs officials.

On that cold January day when I was there, I felt there was a certain numbness and uncertainty in the air: people going about their business, but nothing much happening. As darkness descended down onto St Saviour's Dock I went back down to Bermondsey; peered in through the windows of estate agents *Michael Kalmar* at the bottom of Shad Thames and made some notes on their current offerings. Reader, you could buy a huge loft space at number 174, Tower Bridge Road (Sadlers Lofts, above the Antiques Exchange) for £220-325,000; an apartment at Tyers Gate (newly refurbished warehouse) for £195,000; ground floor of number 145, Bermondsey Street would cost you £187,500; and just a little less, apartments at the Morocco Store in Leathermarket Street for prices from £120,000, and at the Lantern House, Morocco Street, from £115,000. Overcome with incomprehension and no little anxiety I hastened on my way home.

Opposite: *Three Tuns Tavern*, Jacob Street; water-colour drawing by T.H. Shepherd, 1854. Courtesy: Trustees of the British Museum.

Below: *Eckett Street*; a drawing by Sydney Jones, from his book Thames Triumphant, 1943. Now gone, the street was located between Jacob Street and Wolseley Street.

Above: *Vogan's Mill*, built 1989 for the Rosehaugh Co-partnership Development Ltd, designed by Michael Squire Associates (also responsible for the new Tower Bridge Visitors Facilities block). This 15 storey block of flats replaces a white concrete silo. Vogan's Mill was a complex of warehouses used since 1813 by the Vogan family for processing grain. Today's building has a dramatic presence seen from Druid Street, with the Roman Catholic church in front.

94

Above: *The Ship Aground pub*; water-colour drawing, 1890, by J. Appleton. The nineteenth century building of the pub which still stands close to Dockhead Fire Brigade Station, in Wolseley ... Southwark Local Studies Library

Above: *Parker's Row, Dockhead;* drawing, 1876, by J.P. Emslie. Courtesy: Southwark Local Studies Library. The building on the far right is that of Alfred Parker, vehicle builder; Pugin's 1834 Roman Catholic church stands behind. (For history see: *The story of the catholic church in Bermondsey,* by Rev. L.J. Bourdelot, Burn, Oates and Washbourne, 1923).

Above: One of a series of six 20 feet long sandblasted mirrors by Martin Donlin in foyers of *Butlers Wharf residential block.*

# APPROACHING SOUTHWARK PARK AND ROTHERHITHE:
## Bermondsey Wall, west and east, Chambers Street, Alfred Salter Conservation Area

Jamaica Road is the main approach to Rotherhithe, with the new Jubilee station (architect: Ian Ritchie) located at its centre. For the pedestrian this route can seem dreary and monotonous and a much·more varied and stimulating environment can be had by taking the riverside approach: Wolseley Street, George Row, leading to Bermondsey Wall West, Chambers Street leading to Bermondsey Wall East; the Alfred Salter Conservation Area in streets behind Cherry Garden Pier; beyond to Corbett's Wharf, to the Angel, and the excavated site of Edward III's palace.

I walked out one Sunday afternoon for my promenade. It was an early February Sunday; the sky was blue and there was just a glint in the air to suggest that we had left behind the gloom-filled days of the January winter solstice; a January when things for me seemed to have gone haywire; but that February Sunday afternoon everything was still; on a London Sunday people retreat into themselves: lay to rest the anxieties of the week; Sunday is a day for early evening chamber music concerts at Conway Hall in the winter months for me, helping me on and forward into the next week. The urban landscape that Sunday had a very quiet, meditative quality, and I spotted only a few couples and lone individuals about.

I plunged into DOCKHEAD and was amazed at the sheer size of Goodhart-Rendel's 1960 *Holy Trinity Roman Catholic Church*, with the clergy house and convent behind, a complex of buildings replacing those of the 1830's destroyed by World War II bombing. The prettily variegated, decorative brickwork creates a dizzy effect and seems somewhat at odds with the scale of the church. On the gates of the *Italian Building* opposite I noted the organisations within: *Pictures Colour Library*; *Burness, Curlett and Partners* (naval architects), *English World-wide* (specialising in the recruitment of English language teachers for posts overseas); *Ptarmigan Media, GBZ Management* (classical music agents).

Modern housing developments follow and continue into the upper end of Wolseley Street (named after Garnet Wolseley, 1833-1913, field marshal, army reformer and active in the Crimea, Egypt and the Sudan). Looking back up the street from its lower end, one is struck by the jumbled landscape, old and new: the pub *The Ship Aground*, the practise tower of the fire station in the foreground, a curved roof behind, Vogan's Mill, and so on. All around here you find the *LCC Dickens Estate*, blocks named after Dickens' characters. No doubt, as the next century rolls on, such estates will be regarded with the interest which we accord to Victorian establishments today. They look lived in places, where people have put down their roots, Wolseley Street leads into GEORGE ROW and at the Jamaica Road end we discover the delightful *St Joseph's Primary School*. Nearby we glimpse the sculpture of St Michael and a dragon in the courtyard of *St Michael's Roman Catholic Secondary School*. It was brought there some ten years ago from a convent in Kent. The school dates from 1959, an amalgamation of two older schools in Bryan and St James' Streets.

At the top end of George Row, forking to the west, we are in BERMONDSEY WALL WEST. *St Saviour's House* a large white commercial block on the corner currently houses *Ye Old Oak Foods*, *SMC Quality Foods*, and the *Admiral Food Trading Company*. *Providence Tower* is a new residential block, one wall orange, the other grey, with protruding balconies and windows. Beyond lies a large Bellway Homes development called *Butlers Square*, bordering on Jacob Street, with a very spacious garden courtyard, shrubs, plants, and a wooden footbridge over a large expanse of water. *Reed's Wharf* is an old warehouse: some upper windows have had new wooden frames inserted, but the occupants have preferred to continue the life of the old building and have not subjected it to the sanitisation methods we find in Butlers Wharf.

At the CHAMBERS STREET corner one finds a quite attractive new block *Springview Heights*, a development from Albany Homes, with balconies made somewhat unusually from wooden panels. Behind, building work is currently in progress. On the Sunday afternoon I was there everything was still and laid to rest: walls had stopped going up, the skips were digesting their rubbish; anticipatory piles of bricks lay around. A huge red crane hung over the arrested proceedings: a subject of interest to an artist, I thought. Indeed, this thought came to me again as I strolled down Chambers Street, which is dominated by the gigantic blocks of *Chambers Wharf and Cold Stores*, now used for storage by Hays Information Management. Reader: inside there are crates and crates of documents; in places like this, all the endless business of human activity as recorded on paper comes to rest. Again in *Llewellyn Street* an artist's subject appears: the heavily defensive premises of *Gilray Plant Ltd* (suppliers to the scaffolding industry), walls covered with barbed wire, padlocked gates, fire alarms, and non-parking signs. Nearby are the works of *Chamber Motor Services* and *Twyford Commercial Ltd* (commercial vehicle repair), again protected with much barbed wire. At the bottom of *Loftie Street* there is Studio C of the South Bank Studio Centre based in Galleywall Road, and at the riverside end the disused premises of former *Flint Scenery*.

Beyond, one can glimpse the tower of St James' Church; the friendly facade of the old Farncombe Street School comes into view, and we are in a new locality, dominated by Southwark Council and private housing in Bermondsey Wall East around Cherry Garden Pier. An article in Rotherhithe Community Planning Centre's booklet *Our Side of the river* (c. 1985) records how this resulted from a controversial LDDC competition in 1993. At the centre of *Fountain Square Green* there is a somewhat ungainly fountain structure, but as elsewhere, it is non-functional. From here you can pause and take in the panoramic views, much loved by the estate agents, the big Bridge, and over in Wapping, Oliver's Wharf, Wapping Pierhead, the River Police, and so on.

The *Alfred Salter Conservation Area* centres around Janeway Street, Emba Street, and Wilson Grove; it dates from 1928, architects: Culpin and Bowers, and conveys a somewhat suburban mood; doorways are often protected behind semi-circular arches and trees and shrubs are much in evidence. The tensions of inner city life seem to have dispersed as if by magic when one wanders around this small peaceful enclave.

Above: *Works of Messrs Charles Southwell & Co, Dockhead*; from *A Descriptive Account of Southwark and Bermondsey*, W.T. Pike, 1894. The firm were wholesaler and export manufacturers of jams, jellies, marmalade, candied peels, etc; the works opened in 1885 and consisted of 16 distinct buildings.

Above: *Hop Studios, Jamaica Road.* Present-day premises of Spice Design Consultants (previously at the old Hop Exchange). From 1884 to 1970's owned by builders Talbot & Lugg; doors and windows are new, but the brickwork is original.

Opposite: *Pub, now a Liam Og's*, opposite St Saviour's Dock. This stretch of Jamaica Road was formerly known as Dockhead (today a turning just east of Mill Street).

Above: *Christ Church and schools*; from the Illustrated London News, 1849. Architect: W. Bennett Hays; situated in Parker's Row, just north of Abbey Street; demolished in 1967. Photograph of interior, 1923, in SBR, II.

Above: *St Joseph's Catholic Primary School*, 1912; situated in George Row; the building is given character by its busy roof top elevation with chimneys, circular and triangular gables.

Above: *Riverside Primary School*, Bevington Street; built 1874, originally known as Farncombe Street School, and situated next to the Bermondsey Settlement. Different roof top elevation at rear.

The private housing south of Cherry Garden Pier is taller, grander and heavier than the public housing: the roof tops are gabled, the brickwork is bright orange and there are long grey bands; the wooden framed windows have heavy, grey corbels which are not beautiful. This housing is grouped around several courtyards in Marigold Street, Cherry Garden Street and Pottery Street. Southwark Council's neighbourhood housing office at the lower end of Cherry Garden Street is an attractive 1990's structure.

*Corbett's Wharf* was converted in 1983; like Oliver's Wharf across the river this was a very early warehouse conversion. We note the irregular position of the windows, and the ground level       painted pillars, and can tell at a glance that this is a very expensive residence. Artist Lady Rose Cecil was living here at one time in the 1980's. The 1930's block *Angel Wharf* stands opposite. *Millpond Estate* has been subjected to the improvement treatment we find on other estates around here: real regeneration, but the heavy stone entrances are ungainly.

*The Angel pub* is another good place at which to pause, and there is seating at the riverside edge. We can enjoy the old photographs and prints in the bars and read the interpretation panels around the grassed-over excavated site of *Edward III's palace*, part of the Cherry Garden development scheme. By contrast, Bermondsey Abbey foundations were not laid bare after Museum of London excavations, and the Trocette Mansion now stands on the site.

*Kings Stairs Garden* comes next down the riverside, with its central play area, and the Roman Catholic church *St Peter and the Guardian Angels*, 1902, architect: R.W. Tasker, tucked away in a corner. This is another Roman Catholic community: there is a convent here, fronting Jamaica Road, the *Silesian Sisters of St John Bosco* (John Bosco was a nineteenth century Italian priest), and the *Bosco Centre* is a nursery school with evening clubs. Sister Cecile, founder of the centre was featured in Southwark News, Southwark People Series, March 16th, 1995.

The 1980's LDDC competition winning housing in Elephant Lane and Mayflower Street seems tedious in its repetition of angled gables, but the complex is probably typical of its period. Troughton McAslan's white-faced, seven storey block *Princes Tower* at numbers 93-97, Rotherhithe Street has more character, but hardly harmonises with the surroundings and seems to have strayed away from Butlers Wharf. Nevertheless, despite such carpings from an outsider, people do want to live here. Some nine apartments in *Pilgrim House* (initially intended for commercial use) were marketed for prices from £135,000 to £200,000 and 'went' the estate agents claim, within a week (Southwark News, 'Southwark Property' article, February 5th, 1998).

One can wander away from this promenade, sadly perhaps...feeling that we are not living in a very aesthetic age, that architects, like everyone else, are simply doing a job for their clients, who likewise are doing a job. We might reflect that the late twentieth century built environment is now well and truly all muddled up, reflecting only the sheer muddle of the human society within it.

Above: *Number 5, Bermondsey Wall West*, drawing by Hubert Williams. Courtesy: Southwark Local Studies Library. A companion to 'Bridge House' in George Row, both houses feature in Sydney R. Jones' *Thames Triumphant*.

Above: A drawing from the annual report of the *Cambridge University Mission*, 1953/4. Now known as the Salmon Youth Centre, after is founder Rev. H.D. Salmon (of Queen's College, Cambridge) who started a boy's club and public dispensary at 47, Jamaica Road in 1906. The building shown was replaced by a new one in 1956, but the rear part still stands (a plaque reads: 'Cambridge Medical Mission Settlement, 1910').

Above: A drawing from The Leisure Hour, 1895; below: drawings from the annual reports 1892-6. *The Bermondsey Settlement* opened in 1892 in Farncombe Street. Dr Rev. John Scott Lidgett who founded it was warden from 1892 to 1949. Between 1909-18 it was part of the South London Mission, rejoining 1954-67. Scott Lidgett's long association with the area is remembered in a nearby Scott Lidgett Crescent. His bust can be found in the church at the South London Mission. The Settlement closed and was demolished in 1969. A full account of its educational, religious and community work is to be found in John Beasley's *The bitter cry heard and heeded*, 1989.

Here is a short contemporary account of the Settlement, from *Living London*, 1901: "Members are requested not to touch the ceiling with their feet" is the rather startling notice confronting us as we enter the gymnasium of the Wesleyan Settlement in Bermondsey. Short of kicking down the plaster in some acrobatic flight, here are innumerable ways of letting off youthful steam, such as fencing, footballing, cricketing, or enlisting as a modern Knight Templar in the Boys' Brigade. Not only the roughness, but the ugliness of London life is being gradually dispelled wherever one of these wonderful little colonies has been planted. Here in Bermondsey, for instance – on the south side of the Thames, opposite Wapping – we might find a sight to gladden the eyes in the merry month of May: a genuine May-day festival in the Settlement court, the lassies tripping it merrily round the maypole, to the unbounded delight of an audience crowding the very roofs around. For old and young alike, the Settlement is a radiating centre of interest and good cheer.

Drawings from article in the Leisure Hour, 1895, part of its series on
London settlements.

Dining-room
for Residents

Recruits
for the
Boys' Brigade.

Girls' Gymnasium.
Exercise after Biscuit-making.

Cookery class.
"Cold mutton night"

Drawing-room
for meetings etc.

Bermondsey & Egypt
at the British Museum.

For a full biography see: *Bermondsey Story: the life of Alfred Salter* by Fenner Brockway, 1949, reprinted by Stephen Humphrey (1, Cornish House, Otto Street, London SE17 3PE).

**AS SEEN BY " GAL."**

**The Hon, Member for West Bermondsey.**

Above: *The Hon. Member for West Bermondsey, as seen by 'Gal'*; a caricature from the Bermondsey Labour Magazine, November, 1927.

Opposite and below right: *Dr Salter's day dream*; a three piece sculpture by Diane Gorvin just west of Cherry Garden Pier. There is a cat on the wall behind the child. The LDDC plaque suggests that the doctor is dreaming of his child Joyce who died of scarlet fever. Dr Alfred Salter is an important Bermondsey personality of the 1920's and 1930's. He was a much loved doctor, councillor and MP (from 1922). He is commemorated in many ways: the Alfred Salter Conservation Area, Alfred Salter House (off Lynton Road), the Alfred Salter Neighbourhood Housing Office in Spa Road, and Salter road in Rotherhithe.

Above: A Drawing by W.G. Newton, 1910: from *The Doctor* (i.e. Dr Stansfield, not Salter), by Barclay Baron, 1952.

Above: *The 'Manor House', or 'Bridge House', 64, George Row*; a lithograph by Thomas Robert Way (from Reliques of old London upon the banks of the Thames and in the suburbs south of the river, by H.B. Wheatley, Bell, 1899). This early eighteenth century house was demolished in 1948. Southwark Local Studies Library has an attractive etching of the subject by Hubert Williams. Photograph in SBR, II.

Above: *Bermondsey Wall*; etching, 1934, by Nathaniel Kornbluth. This riverside street runs eastwards from the northern end of Mill Street to Cherry Garden, and is a reminder that the locality was originally below high water level. Again the artist conveys a sense of unfathomable obscurity.

# OLD JAMAICA ROAD

This road winds round from Abbey Street, opposite the tall tower block Lupin Point, and into Thurland Road, and St James' Church. Today, it is something of a backwater, whereas before the 1960's it was part of the main route out from Tooley Street to Rotherhithe. Nevertheless, it is the location for two old mission establishments with residential accommodation: the *Bermondsey Gospel Mission* founded in 1864, and the *Cambridge University Mission*, established in 1906, and recently renamed the *Salmon Youth Centre*.

The gospel building on the corner was built in 1931, architects: Murrell & Piggott, having previously occupied nearby sites. Founded by Walter Ryall, a former deep sea fisherman, it occupied premises in London Street (now Wolseley Street) from 1864 to 1898. Walter Ryall's daughter was the famous gospel singer Annie Ryall. She married William Bustin, superintendent 1891-1946, a borough councillor 1903-18, alderman 1915-24 and mayor 1912-22.

The old pub building next door, the former *Lilliput Hall* is now being converted into flats; the new half-timbering makes the building look very spruce and somewhat out of place in the surroundings.

Opposite you find the *World War I memorial* commemorating the fallen of the 22nd battalion of the Queen's London Regiment; two plaques on the planters have appeared recently commemorating Col. C.H. Nice (1912-95), and Col. J.G. Bevington (1903-94). The memorial is incorporated into the wall of the Royal Marines Reserve building which stands on the site of the *old drill hall* (part of it survives in Abbey Street) (photograph in SBR, II).

Beyond old Lilliput Hall lies gloomy *Giles House* with a straggle of shops at street level, then comes the 1956 old Cambridge University Mission building, looking flat, and doubtless cheaply built. Jubilee Line construction work dominates the area by the railway arches, and there are offices for the works beyond.

A dismal place for anyone to live, perhaps, but the landscape broadens out as we turn the bend: we are welcomed by the *Rising Sun pub*, and are sent soaring up to the golden dragon of *St James'* beyond.

Above: *Peter, the fruit and veg man*; a portrait by Rose Cecil, 1980's. The artist writes: "His shop is called George Staples and is on the corner of West Lane and Jamaica Road. They must have been there for years and have a lot of regular customers. He was incredibly kind and patient with me, and I grew to be very fond of him and his wife."

The war memorial (photograph above) stands nearby, and across the road you find the *Two Brewers* pub, with an attractive sign, run by the Fisher family since 1951.

Above: An engraving from the Penny Magazine (of the Society for the diffusion of Useful Knowledge), January 6th, 1836 showing *St James' Church from beneath the viaduct*. An unusual, artistic perspective; note the open carriage on the right, and the bell glass plant containers.

Other engravings show a departing congregation: Phillips' history of 1841 has a near copy of the print drawn by N. Whittock, engraved by R. Winkles, with an awaiting carriage; Walford's Old & New London, 1876 shows the churchyard, with three lamps (drawn by P. Justyne, engraved by R. & E. Taylor).

St James' is one of South London's seven churches built by the Waterloo Churches Commissioners; it was consecrated in 1829. A peal of 10 bells was cast at the Mears foundry in Whitechapel, made from cannon left by Napoleon at Waterloo. The painting of the Ascension of Christ by a one John Wood was chosen from 73 sketches submitted in the 1839 competition (£500 left by John Harcourt, one of the church's founders, in his will for this purpose).

Ruth Kendall's History, 1979, includes old advertisements and a photograph of the dragon taken down for cleaning.

# AROUND ST JAMES' CHURCH

In search of another kind of churchyard atmosphere, I have often made my way in summer months to St James' churchyard in Thurland Road. We owe the churchyard to the efforts of a vicar Dr William Allan who persuaded a Jewish lady Mrs Emma Montefiore to contribute the cost in memory of her late husband Nathaniel, and on the fountain dated 1886 we find recorded that he 'sought to do the maximum of good with the minimum of notoriety'. Opposite there is an obelisk memorial to William and Ann Lucey.

All this is hardly of concern to the kids who play their football games here, do their noughts and crosses on the tarmac, or leave their messages behind on the columns of the portico. Tough youths ride through on their motorbikes; strange looking dogs of many shapes and sizes are brought here for exercise: sausage dogs, woolly brown ones with pink tongues: an artist or photographer should record this strange Southwark canine tribe and owners.

*Doctor David Zigmond* has his surgery in the northern aisle (the southern aisle is also partitioned off). Young and old come to consult the doctor: a daughter wheels in her ageing mother, a schoolboy in a blue blazer hops down the steps with his prescription. Pigeons peck and pick at anything and everything. They squat on the pediment of the church, waiting for the next swoop down. The *Gregorian pub* lies to the east, with an attractive sign and an adjacent lamp, in Jamaica Road, and close by you find many tombstones piled up. The clock in the church chimes out every hour: hollow, ominous, warning us that we all have our time and then that is that.

At the St James' Road side, from 1921 until the early 1990's, you could have found an unusual *covered children's slide*, donated by Arthur Carr, chairman of Peek Frean (see photograph in SBR, II). An article in Southwark News, May 21st, 1992, recorded its vandalisation, and imminent demise; and now it has gone, replaced by a mean, little piece of playground apparatus. What has happened, one may well ask to the generosity of former eras? Could it be that a society that often appears to have given over so wholeheartedly to self-destruction is now deep on its descent into hell? Reader: think for one moment of all the times you have been disagreed with, sat on, pulled to pieces, given a severe verbal lashing, and left reeling almost senseless...
The church clock strikes the hour again: hollow, ominous, warning...

But enough of all this; we must be up and about, exploring the vicinity. In ST JAMES' ROAD, on the corner of Linsey Street we find the *St James' Tavern*; St James is shown with wings and a wooden stick, and the building has three storeys, rounded windows and doorways and decorated pilasters at ground floor level. Opposite St James' Tavern is the *St James' Garden Centre*. Close by in CLEMENTS ROAD, on the corner of Webster Road, there is another large pub *The New Concorde*. In Clements Road you will find a mixture of old and new housing, the extensive Tower Bridge Business Complex (extending to Drummond Road, the former premises of Peek Frean), and with its towering chimney and connecting silver piping the works of *Selkirk*, who design, supply and install chimneys, vents and exhaust systems. Peek Frean closed their factory here in 1989; today they operate from their Leicester and Liverpool sites. In DRUMMOND ROAD we find the *Vineyard Community Church*, between Marden Square and Layard Square. It occupies an old Baptist church building; the congregation was formerly at the 1950's Union Chapel, 155 Tooley Street (the original congregational church was on the corner of Horsleydown Lane and Queen Elizabeth Street). Further up Drummond Road is the Surrey Docks site of *Southwark College*, a former comprehensive school. Beyond the railway road tunnel, to the left, there is BLUE ANCHOR LANE, with its car repair garages, *Fleet Shipping and Packing Services*, established in 1969, and with a Korean speciality, the *Blue Anchor Fish Bar*, and on the corner of Southwark Park Road the *Blue Anchor pub*, dated 1875. Opposite lies a long stretch of flats *Rock Grove Way*. Amidst all this the hardness, the silver birch trees look poignantly fragile and out of place.

Above: *The opening of Southwark Park*, 1869. St James' Church can be seen in the background. The boating lake opened in 1908. An interesting observation of the onset of a shower of rain.

# SOUTHWARK PARK, 1997: recall to sanity and one's natural self? the start of a new era for the park?

Five years on, I find myself still magnetised by this park, going their often during the summer months. Once through the gates, it seems, almost at once, as if all the absurd cares of life have dwindled to nothing: the sturdy plane trees will outlive the flimsy, hollow cars of Jamaica Road, as expendable, as crushable as empty booze cans. In Southwark Park the central questions of one's existence can be faced and perhaps partially answered. The bright red, speckled ladybirds, the little greenbugs, the common dandelions, the creeping groundsel, if interrogated, will all recall us to our real and natural selves.

But on another day, Southwark Park may be a place where you start brooding on whether in fact you, and the whole of society too are in reality sinking: going down, and down, sinking without trace to the absolute unconcern of nature all around. In the children's play area, until very recently, you would have found a sculpture of a screaming head, a hand groping blindly for help; you might well contrast all this with the golden dragon dreaming away at the top of the spire of St James' nearby. The head and hand have now gone, sunk without trace, the gigantic shoe too has vanished, and a mean little play apparatus has appeared. You must not be surprised when locals tell you of nasty goings-on in this park; and in reply, you may well say that society is in decline, is now well into its decadence stage...

Not so, others may say. We want our beautiful park back, say the locals (Southwark News, December 1st, 1993), re-open the lido, clean out the lake, bring back the benches, give us refreshments. A new organisation, Friends of Bermondsey and Rotherhithe Parks now exists and has special concern for this park. A Park Rangers office and visitor centre has opened at the Gomm Road entrance and here you can pick up many colourful information leaflets. An exhibition of improvement proposals was shown here in the summer of 1997: a wildlife sanctuary at the current children's play area, a bandstand on the asphalted circular area, improving the entrances, extending the lake, utilising the old lido, and so on.

The Cafe Gallery too has redevelopment plans, and is currently submitting a lottery funding application to facilitate refurbishing and expansion (Southwark News, November 13th, 1997).

Then there is the old Clare College Mission Church in Dilston Grove, on the edge of Abbeyfield Estate: derelict for many years, its walls have become blackboards for local graffiti; it dates back to 1912 (replacing an earlier church of 1886), architect: J.W. Simpson, and is significant for its use of reinforced concrete: this too may be reutilised in the years ahead. (Profile article in Southwark News, May 1st, 1997).

# ADA SALTER GARDEN: The crows, and the Tibetan refugee

I sat one afternoon in Ada Salter Garden and tried to study my Violin I part of Berlioz Symphonie Fantastique; but the crows were all around; they croak aggressively with hunger pangs; they worry their beaks into empty booze cans, into cracks in the wall, tug stuff out from litter bins; fly off into the tree tops with stuff they have salvaged. Birds can be as neurotic as humans when they are hungry. The crows suffer too from identity confusion, I thought; do not know whether they should frighten the pigeons or be frightened by them; cannot decide how to deport themselves.

And then, that summer Sunday, the Tibetan refugee came in. He came to feed the crows with half a loaf of bread. They all swooped down, all the pigeons and crows and one little sparrow descended onto the Tibetan's white bread offerings. He puffed at a cigarette and told me he had been in Southwark since 1991, that he did paper work, told me that Chinese communists shoot crows dead, told me about Buddhism, and his thoughts about England, and then walked away.

Above: *Lady Gomm House*, a mental health 'resource' centre', run by Southwark Council; situated in Hawkstone Road; built 1885 and formerly the Lady Gomm Cottage Hospital.

Above: Wood engraving by Peter Kennedy, used for poster of the 1991 Bermondsey Artists Group summer show.

Above: A pub sign in Southwark Park Road commemorating Field Marshall Sir William Maynard Gomm (1784-1875). He was Constable of the Tower of London after a military career and was estate owner 1822-75. The Gomm's were lords of the manor of Rotherhithe from the nineteenth century until the 1960's.

Above: *Fountain memorial to Jabez West*; erected in Southwark Park in 1885. He was born in Princes Risborough, Bucks; a farmer's boy, then a fell-monger; from 1838 he was much involved with temperance work in Bermondsey. He died in 1884.

# SOUTH BERMONDSEY: Verney Road, Barkworth Road, Ilderton Road, Zampa Road, Bolina Road, Galleywall Road

It is a strange, remote feeling landscape around here in South Bermondsey, a place well off the beaten track, which doesn't feel like London at all...Not so, of course, say the football fans, this is our place, our home is down here, behind Zampa Road, where do you come from then, mate?...I wandered into the area around South Bermondsey railway station one February evening. I had made my way along Verney Road, chock full of new housing, which would be interesting if there wasn't so much repetition of the same style. On the corner of St James' Road there is the new *Avicenna Health Centre*. Branching into Barkworth Road, I guessed St Bartholomew's church would have vanished. I remembered the desolate landscape when I was there five years ago. I was not wrong: the vicarage building had survived, but the church had been demolished to make way for new housing. Not so, with the 1886 pub, the *Bramcote Arms*, at the end of Barkworth Road; and the *Cliftonville Tavern* – perhaps that had changed its name, I wondered? But not so, it too was still there, facing the Christ Apostolic Church, with the primary school nearby.

Trains sped to and from Central London: station lights, street lamps shone out, cars climbed the slope of Ilderton Road. On the corner of Stockholm Road, I noticed that the building there had originally been Deptford Council Slipper Baths. Today it is called Elite House, and is occupied by *Elite Elevations Ltd* (lift company), and *E & E Scaffolding Services*. *Spicers*, stationery wholesalers have offices down one side of the road; the stadium structure towers over the other side.

Zampa Road leads under the railway bridge to the stadium entrance; car repair works are in the small industrial complex along Bolina Road, and more bridges, rather sinister ones can be encountered beyond. The road narrows considerably at its upper end, and cars sound their hooters not without some alarm. Just beyond the pedestrian tunnel way you encounter some huge, bizarre lumps of stone. What is their origin, or meaning? To the football fans they might symbolise crushing defeat, to the motorist the nightmare of a smash-up perhaps. Reader: I did not want to linger here in Bolina Road that February night contemplating life turned into nothingness, and so got back to Rotherhithe New Road; went up Galleywall Road, past the Victorian school building, past the Manor Tavern, the trading estate opposite, dominated by the Southbank Studio Centre, past the Methodist church, and back into the land of the living of Southwark Park Road.

# Rotherhithe New Road and environs

Rotherhithe New Road is a main road leading from St James' Road at the Old Kent Road junction, northwards past Ilderton Road to the south and Galleywall Road to the north, on to the Hawkstone Road junction, and then beyond to Lower Road. It has its points of interest and sites to discover.

*Bermondsey Trading Estate* lies north of Ilderton Road, by the railway line. A wide range of businesses are listed on the boards; even booksellers Hatchards are here. There is a F.W. Tasker Roman Catholic church, of 1903 in Debnams Road; and close by at the corner of Corbetts Lane the *Jolly Gardeners pub*, its bright green painted ground floor facade, decorated windows, and top storey balustrade (which can be glimpsed from streets around here) communicate a contrasting ebullience and worldliness. The *A.F. Scott* carpet business is close by in a former Royal Arsenal Co-operative Society building of 1933, recorded on a plaque in Silwood Street.

*Silwood Youth Centre* is situated on the ground floor of Lambourne House, of the Silwood Estate. It has several interesting murals: dolphins leaping out of the water, seven children peering over a wall, a motorcyclist on a country road, and another cycling mural adorns the wall around the corner at the entrance to the Silwood Motor Bike Project.

*St Katharine's church* lies opposite in Eugenia Road, a 1960 replacement of the 1884 building; the old derelict church hall, erected 1883, was demolished in April, 1998. The church has zigzagging walls, with honeycomb-type blocks of small hexagonal windows. There are two stone cross memorials in front of the church: to Rev. David Thomas, assistant priest here 1898-1923, and to Hugh Latimer Atkinson.

At the Rotherhithe Old Road junction (opposite Oldfield Grove) you find a rather dramatic, newly painted pub building of 1895, the former *Crystal Tavern*, and now the *London Outreach Centre*. It is a London base of the Arise and Shine Evangelistic Association which has churches in the Philippines and the USA. Its recent advertisement emphasises its problem-solving work (with a biblical/Christian orientation), and Tuesday morning, for instance, is 'encouragement day'. Now, reader this is certainly something we British do not go in for.

Above: *Southwark Park Congregational Church*; built 1859, architects: Morris & Son, it stood on the corner of Hawkstone Road and Rotherhithe Old Road (previously the Commercial Dock Chapel in Derrick Street, established 1800). Lithograph by Whitehead & Morris. Courtesy: Southwark Local Studies Library.

Opposite: *St Anne's, Thorburn Square*, built 1869-70; architect: J. Porter. To the right lies the church hall; Bermondsey and Rotherhithe Housing Association is currently here. Photograph of the square, 1963, prior to demolition in SBR, II. Opposite church, on the other side of Lynton Road lies the Finish pub. Article in South London Press, January 9th, 1998, discusses uncertain origin of the pub's name.

Opposite: *St Augustine's Church vicarage*; a drawing by Martin Millard, 1992. St Augustine's, Lynton Road, was built 1875-83, architects: Henry Jarvis & Son, and is one of London's lesser known monumental churches. The church stands near the St James Road junction, beyond the allotments and the Sultan pub, and is now used by the black ABMT Christian Fellowship. The Architect, 1875, shows the church with the tower which was never built; also illustration in the Builder, 1876.

ST. AUGUSTINE'S VICARAGE, LYNTON ROAD DEL.
©Martin Millard.

Above: *Cliftonville Tavern*, Verney Road, at Ilderton Road junction. The current pub sign shows a man in bathing suit being bitten by a crab, with white cliffs in the background.

Opposite: *Christ Apostolic Church*, 163, Ilderton Road. Previously a Baptist church, erected 1895, architect: George Baines; stands opposite Ilderton Primary School.

Above: *A view from Coopers Road* (off Old Kent Road); drawing, 1992, by Martin Millard. The three blocks are part of the Corporation of London's Avondale Square; the building in front, formerly an old Board school, and in the 1990's an Upper Secondary Support Centre, has now gone. The Windsor Castle pub lies to the south.

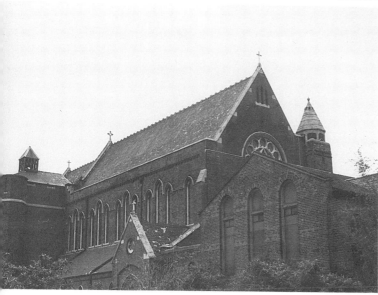

Opposite: *St Bartholomew's*, Barkworth Road, now demolished; built 1866-7, architect: E. Taprell Allen.

# INTERLUDE: IS THERE ANYONE THERE?

Nowadays we all inhabit small worlds very much of our own making; we have all become tiny stumps of identity, seeking out only a clear path ahead, clinging at notions and practises and objects often quite obsessively in a world of complexity beyond comprehension; with the whole world and everything in it reduced to the size of a television screen, we are the lost ones at the end of the century, uncertain in mind and spirit, paralysed into inertia, confused and often distracted beyond belief. We are the lonely, isolated ones at the start of the next century: vast distances seem to separate us all from each other: people living across the courtyard could be inhabiting a town many hundreds of miles away; to walk down the staircase seems like a small expedition; a journey to Rotherhithe and back is like a trek into alien territory. I have sent letters over to Rotherhithe, I have made many telephone calls, but voices from Rotherhithe sound very distant, promised communications fail to arrive. From Bermondsey it seems as if Rotherhithe, or indeed any other London locality is as impenetrable and inhospitable as only England can surely be.

What can bring us all together again? Is there anything at all which can unite us? You will see people in the streets with bibles, with sports bags, which tell us that they are off to participate; yet when it is all over, they will quickly disperse, stray away in splintered, tiny groups, in two's and one's. If conversation starts up, perhaps it goes like this: "So...what do you actually do?"

And the thinking, of course, is: after the money bag, money, as much of it as you can get, it doesn't matter where it comes from, nor what you have to do to get it, but you've got to get money to live.

On my music stand at present there is a great romantic violin concerto, one of the greatest, Brahms, opus 77, of a century ago. This music, too, like all of us today, seems to be saying: 'I am here, I exist, and is all this of no consequence to anyone? The violin writhes, and dances, exalts and despairs, woos and laments, and finally engages in daring athleticism and gymnastic display. We applaud the perspiring violinist, he wipes his brow, he receives his bouquet, and then his well-wishers off stage. But we are not geniuses, most of us, and for us life is a struggle almost until our very final day to simply compel attention, to feel that we are at the centre of a circle, however illusionary.

What is the true significance of our existence? Why are we all here? Perhaps the ultimate significance of things can only be glimpsed by a very few, and they will be people almost impossible to meet, living far away, at a very great distance from society. For most there is only bafflement and a tragic misunderstanding about a very great deal, and a conclusion that selfishness is the only way through and that people will only do anything for money.

Why are we the upside-down, got it all wrong society today? Why are we all so property, and machine and money obsessed today? If indeed our history is drawing to its close, then perhaps only survival sense prevails, there are no longer values, no longer codes of conduct; anything can be blurted out, nothing is worthy of respect any more when all that appears to matter is the survival of 'me'.

Draw apart the curtains, fling open the windows and doors; let in the wind and air; gaze out at the ever-changing, wondrous skies; let everything outside come in: the rain glistening on the metallic vehicles in the street lamplight; the giant sunflowers in summer outside the council block...and everywhere the trees, our steadfast companions; the trees which speak to us at all times of growth, of sturdiness, and of slow unfolding, of life and death and renewal; and above the skies are the stars, and beyond is infinity.

... and we are the survivors, the inheritors at the end of the century, and we are simply here; if we should pause for just one moment and consider everything, consider everything for just one moment, is it possible that we might be awe-struck, enchanted, and perhaps quite unexpectedly grateful...?

Above: *Rotherhithe riverside from Cherry Garden Pier*: etching by Nathaniel Kornbluth, 1934. We note how the boys have their backs turned and we sense the artist's greater interest in the mysterious waterfront vista; no sense of a community is implied here as in the Appleton drawing. The scene depicted is very similar to the photograph, 1953 in SBR, II, and highlights the artist's characteristic topographical accuracy.

Above: *The great fire at Rotherhithe: the scene from the river*; from the Daily Graphic, February 27th, 1894.

Above: *Launch of the Ariel steamer at Rotherhithe*; from the Illustrated London News, April 20th, 1844. Built by John Jenkins Thompson for the Woolwich Steam Packet Company and capable of holding 600 persons.

Above: *Rotherhithe Street from Wapping riverside* (Wapping Police Pier): a coloured etching, 1986, by Peter Chase; a view much favoured by artists, the above has much of the artist's characteristic romanticism and nostalgia.

Above: A drawing by Leonora Ison showing river edge, back view of old houses depicted in Dennis Flanders' drawing. Courtesy: Southwark Local Studies Library.

Above: *Rotherhithe morning*; pastel, gouache, collage painting by David Lockett.
Exhibited at a one-man show 'Thames Paintings', 1995/6 at Greenwich Theatre Art Gallery in 1997; the artist commented: 'I teach art at the John Roan School, Blackheath, and cycle to work along the Thames from Rotherhithe through Deptford to Greenwich. The paintings are about that journey, a mixture of social and natural history, from mist, mud banks, gulls and rotting wharves, to the Babel of Docklands Development, facing Pepys Estate. The riverbank at Rotherhithe, scene of Turner's 'Fighting Temerarire' is watched over by an ever-present heron. I go from an expanse of light on water to the scrap metal yards of Stowage. The imperial history of the Naval College to the congestion of Lower Greenwich! Clouds move over the city from Greenwich Park - to make an equivalent for all this on the picture plane'.

# ROTHERHITHE VILLAGE, September 1997

I was here for several days in late September, resolved at last to penetrate the *Rotherhithe Picture Research Library*. Occupying a former granary building (Grice's Granary), dating from the late eighteenth century, the timber beams from old ships and the low hanging lights give this extensive archive of picture research material a special atmosphere. Established in 1976, and open to all, it is in fact part of the Sands Films studio complex which is also here. The files therefore tend to concentrate on architectural, costume and applied arts subjects of interest to set and costume designers, but at the entrance you will find two shelves of pictures of the locality, Surrey Docks scenes and two files on the diverse specialist areas of dock labour, weddings, portraits, holidays. The southern part of the building (1880 extension) is not in fact a public restaurant, but the firm's catering area for those using the studio and related workshops here. Sands Films, the production company of Richard Goodwin and Christine Edzard is famous for films such as Little Dorrit, and for its design and creation of costumes and sets for the film and Covent Garden production of Tales of Beatrix Potter. Rummaging through these Bermondsey and Rotherhithe files, I would alight from time to time on pictures of interest to me: a laden cart and horse crossing a lock bridge at twilight, Paradise Street in 1938 showing the Ark church, a newsagent's shop in St Marychurch Street, old pubs such as the Sir William Gomm in Abbeyfield Road, a drawing of the Dog and Duck, the previous Three Compasses in Rotherhithe Street, a pub under the railway arches in Rotherhithe New Road, and several interesting aerial views of Southwark Park when the lake was larger, when there was a bandstand to the south, and a view of the entrance when it was known as Paradise Gate.

A talking book was playing when I was there: just me and the librarian there that afternoon. At 4.00pm, closing time, I wandered out into the bright autumn sunshine. I looked around me at this historic riverside village. Could this really be regeneration, I wondered? I read the historical facts concerning the church (*St Mary with All Saints*): the earlier mediaeval church, the present-day church built in 1715, architect: John James; old tower from earlier church replaced in 1748 by Lancelot Dowbiggin. Yet, it seemed to be a place of great, unfathomable mystery: the trees all around spoke of sadness, the fanlights of the windows, the small circular turret of columns, and the tapering spire seemed to be commenting on the eternal roundabout of life, on its vanity and precariousness, a mood very different from the jubilation and confidence of St James, Bermondsey and the squat, eccentric charm of the facade and tower of St Mary Magdalene.

There is mystery and strangeness in the churchyard too: the three pigs' heads on the tomb of eighteenth century Mother Rachel, who jumped to her death from the tower of the old church; the table tomb inscription to Prince Lee Boo, brought back to England by Captain Henry Wilson from the pacific island of Belau where he was shipwrecked in 1783; but the young prince died of small pox the following year; the secluded large tomb, behind locked railings, of Francis Theodore Hay (of Hay's Wharf, and father of Charles Hay, bargebuilder) and his wife; and the new sculpture of Jamie Sargeant commemorating Captain Christopher Jones of the Mayflower are all strange apparitions in this film set location. Mystery and silence surround the rectory too: dating from 1869, architect: R. Hesketh, it is a spacious building with many rooms; a tree of heaven stands between the entrance piers.

*Hope Sufferance Wharf*'s old granary and stable buildings are currently boarded up, awaiting redevelopment, the sign 'Rotherhithe Workshops' the sole reminder of the community workshops, businesses and services which were here for some twenty years; Bermondsey and Southwark News for example had offices in the granary from 1987 to 1995 (it started life as a press agency in 1985). At the other end of St Marychurch Street we encounter the end of another Rotherhithe enterprise: the boarded-up premises of the restaurant *Rogue's Kitchen*, incorporated into the Adam Gardens Estate housing block. The proprietor was Audrey Kilpack and the business started in 1976, previously a docker's cafe from the 1940's.

The *Waterside Co-operative*, at number 99, Rotherhithe Street, is another studio complex. Dating back to 1974 its future is now under threat from the property developers, reports an article in the South London Press, March 27th, 1998.

A small property company Seagers Residential is the current leaseholder of the *Amicable School House*, famous for its stone figures of two charity children (they have yellow stockings, and rather ugly faces), an early eighteenth century building, which from 1795 until the end of the nineteenth century housed the local school founded in 1613 by Peter Hills and Robert Bell. One of the partners spoke to me of his endlessly-frustrated dealings with the local council over the purchase of the 1821 watch-house next door, again boarded up and vandalised. Would it be allowed to deteriorate, he wondered, until eventually it became only a street facade like the 1821 engine house on the other side of the churchyard?

That afternoon the church itself was locked, and I stared in through the glass central doors. I felt as if I was looking in through a museum case (even though the church is thriving and active): copies of old master paintings in panels of the reredos, sixteenth century stained glass showing the Virgin Mary, the four columns, the candelabras, the memorials to mariners on the walls all around and behind in the vestibule, the boards carrying details of charitable benefactions, and an early nineteenth century map.

Above: *An eighteenth century engraving of St Mary's*, published by J. Edington. The doorway to the right has now been bricked up. Several rows of tombstones stand today in the north western corner.

Opposite: Sculpture, by Jamie Sargeant, commemorating Captain Christopher Jones and the Pilgrim Fathers' journey to the New World. Unveiled on July 2nd, 1995 by Hardwick Smith Junior, Governor General of the National Society of Sons and Daughters of the Pilgrims, as part of the 375th anniversary celebrations. (Photograph in Southwark News, July 6th, 1995).

The artist comments:

"Christopher Jones' Christian name prompted an association with St Christopher (from Christophoros - 'Christ bearer', and his mythic role as vehicle of the child Jesus)...his windswept head peers back over his shoulder, perhaps eyeing his ship (and in situ the church of St Mary), or beyond to England and home. He would return there to die a year later at Rotherhithe. The child's open expression faces forward to the New World. His right arm is raised in an expression of blessing/greeting..."

Feeling giddy with so much time, I wandered away; went down *Elephant Lane*, past the premises of the Bubble Theatre Company (now twenty years old), and into the new 1980's housing, a competition-winning project from Corrigan Soundy and Kilaiditi, concluding with the two business blocks Pilgrim House and United House. All these cut-out, angular shapes seemed to be far removed from the mysterious old dwellings I recalled from a 1930's photograph. I stared out through the railings at the roundabout with its horrendous traffic, school children straggling home, and the 1980's City Business Centre (St Olav's Court) with its variety of services and media operations, including Indigo Creative, designers of the Southwark Festival brochures for several years.

It was time to leave all this behind: the instability and anxieties of the past and present, and take a stroll through Southwark Park with its crisp, crinkly leaves, its sturdy plane trees, its frolicsome, innocent grey squirrels and its meditative black crows.

Above: *The organ at St Mary's, Rotherhithe*, built by John Byfield II, 1764-5; the organ gallery survives, but the northern and southern galleries were removed during William Butterfield's restoration. Note the panelled base to the columns on the left.

Opposite: *East India Wharf* (a former granary building), opposite Hope Sufferance Wharf, Rotherhithe Street. Currently undergoing conversion.

Opposite: *Disused London Hydraulic Power Company pumping station*, Renforth Street; a drawing by Martin Millard. Built 1902 and operational until 1977. Chimney visible from Tower Bridge.

I observed in 1992:

The chimney soars upwards; sparrows build nests in the crevices; pigeons squat on the railings above the metal panels; butterflies flit about. This is a building at the end of its history; protected by barbed wire, ugly graffiti is sprawled on the gates and walls. Little kids ride about on their bikes; adults stray home from work, weary, bored, uncertain of their futures. A smart van parked nearby belongs to Melki, computer supplies specialists. Scaffolding stands at the base of the two council tower blocks...

Above: *Stone from Surrey Docks*, Kings Stairs Gardens; unveiled by the Queen on her jubilee visit in 1977. However, it was vandalised and has now gone (see Southwark News, May 25th, 1993).

Above: *Memorial to Edward Blick*, Rector of St Mary's, 1835-67, outside entrance to church. He was especially active in establishing other churches and schools in the area, and is commemorated too by Blick House, in Neptune Street.

Above: Pump, built in 1929, used at *Lavender* Dock Impounding Station until 1969. Now located outside the Brunel Engine House.

Above: *'Sunbeam Weekly and the Pilgrim's Pocket'*; a bronze sculpture by Peter McLean, at Cumberland Wharf (opposite Swan Road), unveiled November 29th, 1991 by Mrs Elsie Marks, vice-chair of the Mayflower Tenants Association.

Above: *Mayflower pub, pre- World War II, riverside facade*; drawing by Joan Bloxam. Courtesy: Southwark Local Studies Library. (To be contrasted with Don Jarvis' 1979 drawing of the present building, which was included in the first edition). Note Church Stairs to the right. This historic pub dating from the mid-sixteenth century features in countless guide books, which often refer to its tradition of selling American stamps. However, new owners Sue Robinson and Ian Roache confess (article in South London Press, December 12th, 1997) to being in a quandary, unable to find them, nor the license to sell them!

To the east of the pub lie: Grice's Wharf, at number 119 (c. 1859); Tunnel Wharf at numbers 121-123 (mid nineteenth century); then a riverside seat area (the giant knots went but new ones have recently appeared, see article in Southwark News, June 4th, 1998); then Brandram's Wharf, at numbers 127-131 (1870-80 warehouse converted in 1985-7); a new development, Hay's Court, is at number 133; and Charles Hay & Co (established 1789) are next door.

Above: *a drawing by Geoffrey Appleton published in 'By peaceful means: the story of Time and Talents, 1887-1987'*
by Marjorie Daunt; also used by the organisation in its other literature. A creative, yet searching community spills out
of a waterside landscape, featuring: a towerblock of the Canada Estate, a gable end of Hope Sufferance Wharf, East
India Wharf (with adjacent crane), a small building once occupied by G. Carr, bargebuilders, and then Thames Tunnel
Mills, former works of White Tomkins and Courage who warehoused and manufactured a wide range of food stuffs;
now converted for residential use by London Quadrant Housing Association in 1983.

# OPEN HOUSE: Visiting some interiors in the City, Bermondsey and Rotherhithe, September 21st, 1997

I picked up the leaflet Open House: a celebration of London's architecture, free entry to over 400 buildings across London (part of the European Heritage Open Days), at the entrance to the Old Operating Theatre and Herb Garret in St Thomas Street one day early in September. Here I thought was an opportunity not to be missed.

And so, on Sunday, off I went; crossed Tower Bridge, and got to St Paul's to penetrate *St Bart's Hospital*: went through the heritage centre with all its pictorial panels and joined the throng crowding up the staircase to view the Hogarth murals and the Great Hall with its portraits and tablets recording benefactions. Going out, I encountered St Bartholomew the Less, previously unknown to me. On to number 68, Upper Thames Street to visit the brand new, prestigious interior of *Vintners Place*: a richly painted ceiling, twinkling lights, marble flooring, Vatican-inspired steps, all cool and silent, and very twenty-first century; then down below ground to gaze in through glass doors at the gym, equipped with all the latest machines, and opposite the swimming pool with its beautiful Italian landscape mural. I and two others concluded that today's fitness obsession must be regarded as a kind of addiction. In the Long Room at *Custom House*, in Lower Thames Street I gazed in horror at the sea of computers, all identified with a personal name, an official stood talking to visitors beside a blow-up engraving of the nineteenth century interior. In the robing room I was interested to find framed photographic prints of East End riverside paintings by Mackenzie Moulten. In the entrance hall there were glass cases containing contraband daggers and knives.

And then to the bridge, yet once again. I crossed over and got to Melior Place to visit the *Glasshouse*, source for me of endless speculation. What did it contain? Now I would know. There was a queue, to my amazement, to get into this fantasy house, converted by interior designer Michael Davis from a former garage and containing a crowded array of mirrors and fantasy sculptures by Andrew Logan. The place buzzed with creative craziness and it seemed as if I had gone right back to the 1960's. I had stood in the queue with a boy about to become a student of civil engineering. I wonder what he thought of this fantasy place.

I had to hurry on, weighed down with my orange carrier bag, to get to Rotherhithe. Here was something, again, quite different. Up St Marychurch Street, glimpsing the Ship (present-day building dates from 1939; sign shows human hand grasping ship on a tropical blue sea), and into the *Old Mortuary*, 1895, architect: Norman Scorgie, now converted into a community centre, the base today of the *Time and Talents Association*. There is a full programme of recreational activities, including a reminiscence group. Two small meeting and activity rooms were open. More leaflets, more publications to buy (historical accounts; a guided walk, a 1996/7 sociological survey), more artefacts. An attractive mosaic mural of Tower Bridge and Canary Wharf hung on the wall in one room, original artwork by Geoffrey Appleton for the history of the organisation was propped up in another room displaying artefacts made by the art class. Another mosaic for a location near the entrance was in preparation, I was informed.

At the 1842 *Brunel Engine House* in Tunnel Road I lingered over the interesting illustrations, one showing a girl on a tightrope in the tunnel, an advertisement for fresco paintings of British and continental views by a one I.B. Menkin, stared in through a glass case at a little booklet called 'Sketches of the works for the tunnel under the Thames from Rotherhithe to Wapping', 1828. Below, in the centre of this heritage building opened in 1980 is a pumping engine of 1885 by J. & G. Rennie last used in Chatham Yard. On going out, more leaflets, more publications, and I was persuaded to part with £1.99, special offer, for a 1992 book *Brunel's Tunnel and where it led*, by Andrew Mathewson and Derek Laval. The 80 foot diameter shaft, erected in 1825 standing next to the engine house was used for tunnel construction and then adapted as the pedestrian staircase used between 1843 and 1869.

The final open house place to visit was the *Rotherhithe Youth Hostel*. In the entrance foyer to the left there is a sequence of colour photographs showing the Queen opening the building in March 1993, shaking hands, chatting, signing a book. I peeped in at the Mayflower Restaurant, and the lounge, and was given a key to Room 119. To my surprise, I found six bunk beds. A print of Buckingham Palace was on the wall. I gazed out through the window. A youthful visitor might get very first impressions of the big city from a window like this: down below at Surrey Commercial Wharf you will see Blunn Slates, and John Williams & Co, roofing specialists, established in 1870. Beyond the bascule bridge lies Whitbread's gigantic riverside pub Spice Island. As I departed, international youth bounced about in casual wear; far away from home, their lives had hardly begun.

I went back down Rotherhithe Street; saw the backs of gigantic armchairs in the bay windows of expensive new properties, trendy children's toys, rows of potted plants, and wondered, no doubt like so many others, what it was that all these new residents had actually done, or were actually doing, to earn so much money. Returning from Rotherhithe to Bermondsey I strayed into the Angel pub, surveyed the framed photographs, mainly of the 1930's showing old streets, made some notes, and scuttled away.

That day, the Open House day, I returned to Bermondsey realising that I had been to some interesting interior spaces; the day before I had been to Camberwell, had been amazed at the interior of St Mary's Greek Cathedral, had wandered through a private house called Camberwell Hall, had climbed the hill to Grove Chapel, with its cool, silent interior.

All these places were interior places, places that communicated a sense of what was within: the communal and private concerns and obsessions of city dwellers. I returned to my own little bolt hole, looked at all the accumulated stuff, and wondered what it all actually communicated about my own inner self.

Above: *Eighteenth century houses (east of the Angel pub) in Rotherhithe Street before demolition*; a drawing by Dennis Flanders published in the Illustrated London News, 1960 (reproduced courtesy: ILN and Dennis Flanders). Number 51, the Jolly Waterman pub is shown next to Queen's House, originally a mission of Queen's College, Cambridge, and later 1941-53 run as a community centre by Time and Talents. The chimney is that of Gillman and Spencer's mill, and the brick wall on the far right that of Park Buildings. Other pubs once stood in the vicinity: the Dover Castle at number 39, the White Lion at number 85 and the Torbay at number 91. This stretch also drawn by Frederick Moody (his London in Pen and Ink Series, No. 44, What's on in London, May 8th, 1964).

# SCANDINAVIAN FORAY

The Jamaica Road approach to Rotherhithe may well be bleak and ugly, but it affords a long range view of *St Olav's Norwegian Church* (with Canary Wharf rearing up behind). Its position beside the Rotherhithe Road Tunnel, at the top of Albion and Brunel roads is so commanding that one could mistake it at first for a town hall building. Erected in 1927, (with some ancillary rooms at the eastern end built 1995-6), architect: John L. Seaton Dahl, it conveys a sense of civic pride, a flag flying from a balcony in the tower, and a bell-shaped spire with a golden Viking ship weathervane. The elegant wrought iron gates incorporate a bell-shaped motive; there is a relief bust of King Olaf VI on his 80th birthday (unveiled by himself) and the area in front was named St Olav's Square in 1990. A church, we may conclude, which seems celebratory, yet which is also commemorative of human tragedy: 2,101 Norwegian seamen lost during World War I; and a stone pillar records this in English (words not easily legible). There is more King Olaf inside (Olaf II, St Olav, 1015-1030): in the foyer there is a splendid black statue (a copy of the original at Norway House, Trafalgar Square, made in 1921 by Gustav Laeram), and in the church he joins the apostles and Martin Luther in a gallery of stained glass of great distinction. The establishment is interesting as it combines community and church functions with a large lounge/meeting room in front as you enter, and the church with its very different atmosphere behind. The oak panelling, the large array of pink chairs, prints and paintings all around the walls make the lounge a place of purposeful, yet relaxed social dealings, to read newspapers and eat meals, and an ideal venue for the annual Christmas bazaar. There is a painting of the church exterior, 1993, by Arne Waerstad, and the folklore prints are by Terje Grostad. The church, also oak panelled, has a model of a Norwegian ship St Olav hanging from the ceiling. In an adjacent office area you can be shown the stained glass (the last Supper) from the organisation's first church, the Ebenezer Church in Redriff Road (now the Docklands Settlement). A bell from the first church hangs over the entrance to the lounge.

Just behind St Olav's we find the *Finnish Seamen's Church*, built in 1958, architects: Yorke, Rosenberg and Mardall (who also designed the adjacent Civic Centre, 1975). Its bell tower is a prominent landmark. The organisation started off from a corrugated iron church in Plough Way. It was here from 1894 to 1910 when it was sold for £25. It moved to Branch Road, at the Stepney end of the Rotherhithe road tunnel, and stayed there until 1958. The Finnish Church Guild was established in Rotherhithe in 1965, and it is today an important, nationwide networking social and cultural organisation. An illustrated book *100 years of the Finnish Seamen's Mission in London* (in Finnish and English) was published in 1982. The church is plain, a cross carved out of the stone panelled wall, and lighting is in little clusters of circular bulbs. On the upper floor, behind the church there is a cafe, and reading room with a shop. When I was there I heard the clear, hard sound of a Finnish hymn accompanied by piano coming up from the church below: yet again, a sudden panic attack of identity confusion, and I went on my way.

The *Swedish Seamen's Church*, the smallest establishment of the three, is less centrally located, down Lower Road next to the Prince of Orange pub, opposite the police station. It stands on the site of the first Rotherhithe library, and the present-day structure is a rebuilding of 1965-6. The establishment provides accommodation and meals, and the attractive church is at the rear: tall backed seating, and elegant, boxed lighting clusters. From adjacent streets and from Southwark Park you can see the belfry and spire with weather cock.

Although located in Rotherhithe, all three establishments play an important role in the London-wide Scandinavian community. They are bright, purposeful, civilised places; in comparison many a British establishment seems secretive, muddled, and uncertain.

Opposite: *Swedish Seamen's Church, Lower Road.* Note the coloured glass around the door and the anchor to its left.

Above: *Construction of the Rotherhithe Road Tunnel*; water-colour, c. 1908 by Victor Prout. Courtesy: Southwark Local Studies Library. An interesting study of slave-like, yet possibly satisfying physical labour.

From ROTHERHITHE ROAD TUNNEL we have an unusual perspective on the locality: two long pedestrian stairways are graced at street level with ornamental metal structures and from down below, Brunel Road appears as a row of trees; the towers of the two churches in Albion Street take on a new look. The walls are white and grey, orange lights line the tunnel and the inscription above the entrance recording the opening in 1908 by the Prince of Wales (George V) brings back to ones consciousness the traumatic, unresolved tragedy of last summer. Is it possible that the world will for ever more see a road tunnel as a place of the utmost dread? A place which is truly a nowhere place...

ALBION ROAD leads us past the *Neptune pub,* present day building dating from 1894, and onto more mythology at the end of the street where we find the little known *Adam and Eve pub,* with the inscription 1913, Wenlock Brewery Co Ltd beneath the gable, with its two low chimneys and unattractive sign. In between there is the *Rainbow Chinese Restaurant,* the *Convenience Store,* and the Victorian *underground station* building, 1884 with its appealing facade.

BRUNEL ROAD also has its pubs: the *Albion* at one end, and the *Lord Nelson* (here since 1838) at the Canon Beck Road junction. This is a four storeyed building, its ground floor exterior painted bright yellow and green, and happy, relaxed jazz was playing when I was there one March Sunday. The *Little Crown,* by way of contrast, is now boarded up. Also in Albion Street is the *Albion Primary School* nearby, and across the road the *Finnish Seamen's Mission,* modern terraces, a job centre, and a health centre, which expanded in 1996 when a new extension was built.

Above: *Rotherhithe entrance to the Thames Tunnel:* an illustration from the London Illustrated News, 1843. Other illustrations featured Brunel at the rear of a procession of musicians and flag wavers; and the same procession descending the staircase, on the occasion of the tunnel's opening.

The building of the world's first underwater tunnel was an immensely protracted operation: construction commenced in 1825 with the sinking of the Rotherhithe shaft; work ceased between 1828 and 1835 due to lack of finance; the tunnel finally opened in 1843 with government financial assistance. Initially used by pedestrians and stall holders, it was converted into the East London branch under-ground railway line 1865-9. You can see a fine portrait of Sir Marc Isambard Brunel, (1769-1849), by Samuel Drummond in the National Portrait Gallery. He came to London in 1799 from New York and married Sophia Kingdom. His son Isambard Kingdom Brunel was resident engineer.

Opposite: *Rotherhithe underground*: a drawing by Don Jarvis (from his Souvenir of Rotherhithe No 2).

# ANOTHER DAY IN ROTHERHITHE:
## Marbles, hooks, and the Queen's wedding cake:
## a visit to Rotherhithe Heritage Museum

The journey down to the museum is a long way down Rotherhithe Street beyond the village area. This riverside stretch is important historically for the shipbuilding and repair sites which were here until the mid nineteenth century; some twelve sites are carefully documented in Stuart Rankin's booklet *Shipbuilding in Rotherhithe*: an historical introduction and in Stephen Humphrey's chapter 'ship building and ship breaking in his *The story of Rotherhithe*: both make meticulous use of surviving records, giving perhaps an academic stamp to a long vanished Rotherhithe. Today, the area is packed solidly with new housing, most of which comes from some Barratt's. The *Prince's Riverside* development was opened in October 1996. A special event was staged to celebrate Barratt's achievement in the area with Sir Laurie Barratt presiding and reported in a double page feature in Southwark News, October 27th, 1996. After Prince's Riverside come the *King and Queen Wharf* and *Sovereign crescent*: the long, monotonous street facades are deceptive as courts lie behind, named after palaces, and monarchs respectively. In between there is *Globe Wharf*, a large grain warehouse, and later a rice mill, built in 1883, and now being redeveloped by Berkeley Homes. The King and Queen Granary, erected in 1822 was just upstream, and was equally massive. All this redevelopment is perhaps best enjoyed from across the river (from Shadwell Pierhead, or from Waterside Gardens for example) at twilight or night time when the place is sparkling with lights in a way it never was years ago. But to return to our trek: you are at the museum finally when you reach Lavender Road, just before the old 1903 fire station, now converted into flats.

*The Pumphouse Educational Museum* includes the Heritage Museum to the right as you enter; a door to the left on the upper floor of the educational section leads out into the nature park. An LDDC interpretation panel describes the flora and fauna and it is a pleasant place to relax after studying the objects and displays in the museum. The displays are based around the objects found by local man *Ron Goode* on the Thames foreshore. You can see him at his engrossing hobby in a large photographic cut out. I wandered around for several hours, I had the place all to myself; studied reconstruction drawings, photographs and old engravings: a 1717 view of Howland Dock with the mansion house and rows of protecting trees (brought back again into today's redevelopments), Daniell's view of some 100 years later, 1813, showing the emerging dock complex, with Russia Dock in the background. A quotation from Dickens's Our Mutual Friend was put before us: "Rotherhithe...where the accumulated scum of humanity seemed to be washed from higher ground, like so much moral sewage, and to be pausing until its own weight forced it over the bank and sunk it into the river." This wouldn't please the locals, I thought, but Dickens must have sensed a certain lassitude and torpor about the place to have written these words. I recalled the times I had returned from Rotherhithe, emptied of all sense of purpose, with nagging anxiety, longing only to rest my weary head, after a cold refreshment. Ron Goode has collected some 4,000 clay pipes from his scavenging, and the museum displays a selection of them; there are also glass bottles of varying kinds, small toys, trade tokens, coins, buckles and jewellery. There is a small display on *Peek Frean* in Drummond Road from 1866, and a large central display shows all the paraphernalia of dock work: trolleys, weights, sacks, axes and hooks in cases, and photographs of hardwood timber handling at *Vitak's*, timber merchants in Rotherhithe Street until the 1980's.

Departing from the museum, and from the nature park, you will find nature looking much less natural in the 1980's housing at *Heron Place* and *Bywater Place* with its sea of obsessional triangles, intermingled with trees, shrubs, paving stones, archways. The housing diminishes in size as you penetrate within. Not a single person was about when I was there, and indeed perhaps this was how the architects had planned it all: regeneration meaning only filling empty spaces with patterns; after all this occurred at a time when selfishness was supreme, when society had ceased to be. Opposite, between Codrington Court and Pennington Court you can study a segmented obelisk, approached by a set of sloping steps. Beyond, across the river you can study the more monstrous developments of Limehouse and the Isle of Dogs. The final new Rotherhithe Street development site is *Pageant Crescent*, hidden behind a high wall, with turret and cupola.

That afternoon, with absolutely no-one about, after the museum, the foreshore, with the tide out, and with its crazy jumble of lumps of stone, broken brick, pebbles and wreckage looked far more enticing. Seagulls poked about at the water's edge. Gingerly, I went down the wooden flight of stairs next to the converted *Canada Wharf* warehouse, and thought I too could scratch around. I pocketed pebbles of varying sizes and colours, hard little beans and peanuts, quickly was on to metallic finds, wedges, hooks and relics from riverside labour now memories locked in old men's heads, or else turned into heritage museum tableaux.

Buildings, of any kind, of any period surely respond to all this randomness and natural chaos and the repetitive decorative brickwork and rows of lozenge windows of *Canada Wharf* and *Columbia Wharf*, late nineteenth century warehouses nearby, assert the ordering hands of humans. Canada Wharf has now been converted and the 46 flats are now all sold. Columbia Wharf is now part of Holiday Inn.

Wrought iron gates, too, bring us back into the land of the civilised living; the gates outside *Nelson House* should be noted, and further down Rotherhithe Street past the Trinity Business Centre (the site currently awaits redevelopment), the entrance to *Surrey Docks Farm* is a delight to encounter: a duck and bulrush, sheep, pig, cockerel, goat and cow have all been lovingly fashioned.

Above: a drawing by Don Jarvis, 1979 (from his Souvenir of Rotherhithe No 2) of the *iron bascule bridge, Rotherhithe Street,* over entrance canal to area now known as Surrey Water (formerly Surrey Basin of Albion Dock). Another, similar red painted bridge is over Greenland Dock, behind the shopping centre. The Southwark News March 6th, 1998, had a short article: 'Final act of LDDC: Surrey Docks bridges being cleaned up. To the west lies the new pub Spice Island (profiled in Southwark News, August 24th, 1995), and by the river an airshaft of Rotherhithe Tunnel, and beyond the transformed Clarence Wharf Jetty, built 1882 by the South Metropolitan Gas Company and redeveloped by Bellway Homes (see article in Docklands News, October 1997).

136

*Above: Boat/barge builders yard (unidentified), Rotherhithe St; water-colour drawing by James Lawson Stewart, 1880's. Courtesy: South London Gallery.*

Above: *The youth hostel at Island Yard, Salter Road.* Built 1991, architects: Alan Turner Associates, and funded totally by the YHA. It is a large establishment, with conference facilities and restaurant open to the local community. An article Southwark News, November 5th, 1992 reported a successful first year.

Opposite: *Dockland Settlement, at far end of Rotherhithe Street;* opened in 1871 as a Norwegian Seaman's mission, and taken over by the Dockland Settlement movement in the 1920's . Social and sports clubs are based here, but there are plans to make the place into a fully developed community centre. Note the LDDC plaque on the door of the former chapel.

Opposite: *Lavender Dock Pumping Station,* now housing the Heritage Museum, built in 1930 to regulate water levels in Surrey Docks. Also shown is the new nature park and an interpretation panel can be glimpsed on the left.

138

Below: *St Katharine's Eugenia Road*, off
Rotherthithe New Road; built 1884; architect:
W.C. Milne; replaced by new church in 1960,
architects: Covell, Matthews; abstract stained glass
is by W.T. Carter Shapland.
Two stone cross memorials stand in front of today's
church: to assistant priest Rev. David Thomas,
1898-1923, and to Hugh Latimer Atkinson (died
1916).

Above: *World War 1 memorial in Holy Trinity
churchyard.*

Below: *The first Holy Trinity Church,* Rotherhithe Street,
built 1837-8; architect: Sampson Kempthorne; bombed
and replaced by new church, 1959, architect: T.F. Ford.
Noteworthy for its crucifixion mural, 1960, by Hans
Feibusch. A Friends of Holy Trinity, Rotherhithe
organisation was formed in 1996 for the maintenance
of the church and its environs. Former Rev Peter Maurice
profiled in Southwark News, November 21st, 1996.

Above: *St Crispin's, Southwark Park Road*; built 1958-9,
architects: Coe & Robinson. A striking mural by Hans
Feibusch commemorates St Crispin, patron saint of shoe
makers and the ceiling is decorated with a cloudscape by
Phyllis Bray; stained glass depicts the old Christ Church in
Jamaica Road.

TRINITY CHURCH, ROTHERHITHE,

*Consecrated* 1838.

Above: *Nelson Dry Dock, and old Georgian house:* a drawing by Sydney Jonés, from the Sphere.

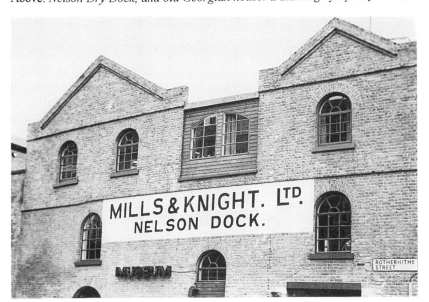

Above: *The former steam engine house of about 1900.*

The Nelson Dockyard complex (facing Canary Wharf) is an historically important site, with shipbuilding and repair activity from the late seventeenth century until 1968. Its story is told in Stuart Rankin's booklet *The Nelson Dockyard*. Mills and Knight were owners from 1890-1960 and Rye-Arc Ltd from 1960-68. The site consisted of slipways, the engine house, the 1740 Nelson House, and Nelson Dry Dock. A French naval training 1952 barque (now called 'Traders Bistro') stands in a slipway, and Holiday Inn (previously Scandic Crown Hotel) has two blocks on either side of the dock (now filled with water). The hotel, opened in 1991 and also occupies adjacent Columbia Wharf. There are 368 bedrooms, a conference centre, fitness facilities (the 'Active Club'). The hotel won an 'Investors in People' award in 1997 for the quality of its staff training. (There are some 2000 Holiday Inns world-wide).

# A CEREMONY AT BARNARD'S WHARF

**10th July, 1992:**

"You are invited to the ceremony on Friday at 11.30 am" Philip Bews, the sculptor from Runcorn told me on the telephone late one evening. You can read the story of ship building activity at Barnard's Wharf - the Barnards, and earlier the Wells, and Thomas Stanton in Stuart Rankin's booklet *Shipbuilding in Rotherhithe - Greenland Dock and Barnard's Wharf, 1997*. Today, Barnard's Wharf is a newly landscaped riverside walk adjacent to Surrey Docks Farm, initiated by former LDDC landscape architect Fraser Broadwick. It is significant today on account of its procession of sculpted animals: fox and dog by Marjan Wouda; two goats and two kids by Althea Wynne; barn owl and mouse (both on walls), by Nathan David; three geese and a cat, by Diane Gorvin; a donkey, two pigs and two piglets by Philip Bews. All these subjects are documented in a LDCC panel.

A little ceremony had been arranged to celebrate these newly made pieces. It was a strange occasion. I found the place at last. There were little groups of people of various ages and backgrounds standing around. I felt almost like an intruder, attending a function that was not intended for me. I found two of the artists: Philip Bews and Diane Gorvin, with their parents and friends from the North-West, looking slightly bemused by their surroundings. Top brass people from the LDDC were there too. People from the local housing estate were there: brand new people in brand new houses; somebody wanted to complain about the railings. Vivaldi came out of the loudspeaker. We were summoned to the official opening: actor Fraser Hines (from Emmerdale Farm TV soap) had come to unveil a plaque. Then we all lined up for dinner in a marquee. Two people behind me spoke worriedly about the problems of finding work, of how to make money. Eventually I was fed, I took my plate and glass and sat looking at Cascades, the architectural extravaganza from CZWG architects, on the Isle of Dogs.

*Return visit to Barnard's Wharf:*
Five years on: the animals are still there; they have not been vandalised. To the south at Commercial Pier Wharf: a gigantic red crane, laid to rest on four pillars, and close by in Odessa Street the Downtown Restaurant.

Above: *A family of pigs, sculpted by Phillip Bews,* with the Isle of Dogs in the background.

# INTO FARMLAND: Surrey Docks Farm

Surrey Docks Farm is a Rotherhithe success story, and an important influence on the urban farm movement nationally. It dates back to 1975 when Hilary Peters brought some goats and two donkeys to waste land at the entrance to Greenland Dock. Today it occupies part of the site of the Wells' yard, where warships and East Indiamen were built 1703-1798. Despite a major funding crisis in 1993 when Southwark Council almost withdrew its funding, but capitulated in the face of a huge campaign and demonstration of protest, despite a fire a year ago, the farm is a thriving establishment today, receiving many visitors. School children have access to fully equipped class rooms and courses are run for people with learning difficulties; produce is sold.

It is perhaps unusual for a farm to incorporate artistic creativity. As you enter the complex to the left you find the workshop of blacksmith Kevin Boys; he runs courses and his creative metalwork is on display at the far. He was featured in a double page article in Southwark Sparrow, October 30th, 1992. A mosaic mural of farm animals (using objects such as buttons and pebbles) can be seen on the wall of the reception area and class rooms; it was created by Jessica Perry, artist in residence with children from eight schools in October 1993. Farm animals are also depicted in a fanlight in one of the class rooms, designed by Susan M. Cook, with the animals lit up by symbolic sun rays. Another mural is planned for the fencing between the compost heaps and the wildlife pond. Kevin Herling will be the artist responsible and it will show the processes of decomposition and recycling in nature.

The main buildings (which include a cafe, a yurt, a bee room) surround an animal yard, with orchards and paddocks to the west. Vegetables are grown on ground by the riverside walk and to the south there is a wild life area with pond. Passing this area and beyond the gate you are met with animals from the farm coming home. At least that was my immediate impression when I encountered the sculpted pigs, geese, donkey and goats: the group of sculpture I came to see when newly made from five years back. Indeed, looking across at the hard, barren world of the new buildings on the Isle of Dogs, and considering the political world that brought all this about, they are quite right to regard the farm as a secure and idyllic haven where very different people are in charge.

Above: *Entrance gates to Surrey Docks Farm:* the sculpted animals were made during a nation-wide festival of blacksmithing here in 1993. The head of the goat has been removed for repair.

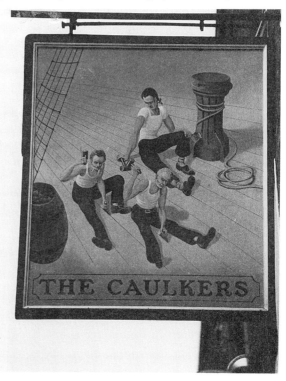

Below: An interesting pub sign, close to Surrey Quays tube station; a pub has stood here since the mid nineteenth century; previously known as the Jolly Caulkers it once had a sign painted by Cosmo Clark showing three less individualistic, but more industrious workers. Today's building has a tall chimney, and the gold lettering, on blue, is lit up by coloured lights.

Above: *The first Rotherhithe Public Library* at 120, ·Lower Road; from Southwark Annual, 1894; architects: Stock, Page and Stock. Courtesy: Southwark Local Studies Library.

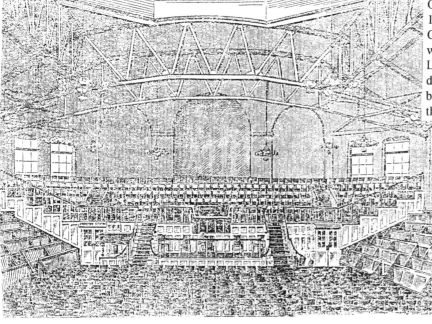

Opposite: *Rotherhithe Great Hall* opened October 1906, the second building of the Rotherhithe Free Church (i.e. free seats). From 1887 to 1905 the church was in a temporary iron church behind numbers 44-48, Lower Road. The church's pastor Thomas Richardson drew huge congregations to his services. Today's building on the corner of Culling Road was erected in the early 1960's.

# LOWER ROAD

Lower Road runs from the Jamaica Road junction, south past St Olaf's Court business complex, and Southwark Park to Surrey Quays Shopping Centre and underground station, on towards Deptford, changing its name to Evelyn Street at the Croft Street/Bestwood Street junction. It is an unusual main thoroughfare with a strange variety of buildings, and it can be perambulated with interest: public buildings, pubs, churches, shops, housing estates, terraces.

The northern, upper end of Lower Road conveys conflicting emotions: of lassitude and retirement from life, energy and activity. The *Rotherhithe Evangelical Free Church* stands on the site of the bombed Rotherhithe Hippodrome; set back from the main road, it has a mood of sadness and withdrawal, enhanced perhaps by the proximity of funeral directors *F.A. Albin in Culling Road.* The present day owner Barry Dyer was featured in Southwark News' Southwark People series (July 17th, 1994). 'I was conceived a funeral director' he claims and states that his favourite place in Southwark is Culling Road, his home and business. Close by is the site of *St Olave's Hospital.* The older, nineteenth century part has now been demolished, replaced by Crest Homes' Parkside development. The site overlooking Lower Road is now the St Olave's House Nursing Home; St Olave's Gate House is occupied by Lewisham and Guy's Mental Health NHS Trust, and the block behind by the London Ambulance Service.

There is more retirement from life at the *Helen Peele Memorial Almshouses,* seven two storeyed homes, with garden in front, erected in 1901: a plaque records the benefaction: 'provided by a trust, under the will of Charles John Peele, a partner in the firm of Brandram Bros. Company of Rotherhithe, in memory of his mother Helen Peele'. There is an attractive strip of iron railing and a notice in French, Swedish and German forbids our intrusion. Brandram's had their works close by across the road for many years until closing in 1958; they produced whitelead, saltpetre and sulphur.

A certain silence and withdrawal also pervades the three blocks of flats in *Moodkee Street,* erected by the South Metropolitan Gas Company in 1931, and at *Orchard House,* opposite the leisure centre.

*Langdon Villas* a nineteenth century terrace leads to the *Seven Islands Leisure Centre;* by way of contrast a place for the fit, active and healthy, or those wishing to be so; its noisy facade incorporates an abstract mural of waves, sky and sea, designed by Rita Harris. It was commissioned by LDDC in 1992. Rita Harris currently teaches Tai Chi Chuan at the Time and Talents centre; she makes semi abstract water colour paintings inspired by this work, by nature and landscape. The leisure centre dates from the 1960's and the Southwark Council crest with its motto 'prosunt gentibus artes' (may the arts of the people flourish) is proudly displayed on the exterior. A new gym, with state of the art equipment, sauna and steam room, dance studio and new cafeteria were opened recently.

There is more blue in the brightly glazed police station. There is light and purpose at the Seamen's Swedish Church, and conviviality at old, long established pubs: the grandiose *Prince of Orange* next door, *China Hall,* with its array of old photographs (here with this name since 1776), and beyond the *Jolly Caulkers* (here with this name since 1784). *The Cock and Monkey* is in Neptune Street.

At the Hawkstone Road junction there is a dramatic increase in commercial activity, and a jumbled, ever changing array of shops and businesses can be studied with some interest: beyond the underground station (with a wall of brick patterned squares), for example, you find (as at February 1998): estate agents *Burnet, Ware & Graves, Roberts Driving School, The Pantry,* sandwich bar, estate agents *Alex Neil,* clothing shop *Jay's Stores.* This business must occupy pride of place in the locality; founded by Alfred Jay in 1950 it has always traded from this site. Across the road you will find *Surrey Docks Pub* and *Raceways Motorcycles* on ground floor premises of the sprawling *Osprey estate,* with its repetitive balcony decoration. Approaching the Plough Way junction you will find estate agents *Oliver Jacques,* the *Cycle Shop* (with a large, rusting old clock above), *Muttleys pet foods, Venezia Pizzeria Ristorante, Goggle Box* (TV sales and repairs), *T.W. Personnel employment agency* (nurses, cooks, domestics, cleaners, etc), and *Diamond Cut* (hairdressers, body piercers and retail jewellers). Opposite on the corner of Rotherhithe New Road you find the circular premises of pawnbrokers *Harvey and Thompson.*

Two nineteenth century pubs, the *Dreadnought* (dating back to 1848), and the attractive *Farriers Arms* come at the start of a residential strip; Stanley Terrace (of about 1830) leads down to the currently boarded up *Merry Cricketers* on the corner of Bestwood Street. The upper floor has been converted to residential use, the ground floor awaits new tenants, with estate agents *Claire & Co* in the northern corner. There are 1980's developments across the road: *Melville Court* (which contains the *Sunny Medical Centre,* and a drugs rehabilitation clinic), a tall, red-framed business block opposite on the corner of Croft Street, with the *Cannon Wharf Business Centre* behind (44 units occupied mainly by computer firms). Across the road there is a branch of *McDougals Restaurants,* occupying a large site, its 'M' logo proudly displayed. We are now in Evelyn Road, in another locality and another London borough.

Above: *Rotherhithe Town Hall, Lower Road;* architects: Murray and Foster; a drawing from Building News, September 20th, 1895. The town hall opened in 1897, but became the public library in 1905 (town hall for the new borough of Bermondsey then at Spa Road); after bombing was at 18, Lower Road (former Salvation Army hall) for 30 years, before moving to new building in Albion Street in 1975 (Rotherhithe civic centre). Two interior views - public hall, and council chamber are included in SBR, II. The exterior is characterised by its doorway, sculpture and profusion of turrets, urns and finials.

Above: *One of the two 'caryatids'* (female figure used as an architectural support) *from the old Rotherhithe Public Library*, sculpted by Henry Poole in 1897. This strange relic is located, somewhat off course and probably completely ignored, in a council estate just behind the Crossways United Reformed Church in New Kent Road. (There is another on the other side of the wall)

*Above: All Saint's Church, Lower Road,* an engraving by William Spence, 1840; built 1840, architect: Sampson Kempthorne; stood opposite St Olave's Hospital; now demolished. The engraving is a charming picture of a then semi rural locality.

Above: *Rotherhithe Public Baths and Washhouses*; from the Builder, February 19th, 1881. The architects George Elkington & Son were also responsible for the Leather Exchange building (which still stands): both have comparable corner turrets. The Seven Islands Leisure Centre (in a very contrasting style) occupies the same site (corner of Gomm Road, in Lower Road).

*Above: The central area of Surrey Quay's shopping centre; a 1998 pencil drawing (especially commissioned) from the sketch-book of Oscar Romp. The view is from the south eastern corner. The artist conveys the chaotic, busy interior with great skill; the figure grasping a glass panel seems lost in his own world, apart from the shoppers and the leaping dolphins (sculpted by David Backhouse) below.*

# BUY, BUY, BUY: Surrey Quays Shopping Centre

'Dreadful', prognosticates Stephanie Williams in the first edition of her architectural guide 'Docklands'. Yet, the locals do not seem to mind this building too much with its coloured brickwork, glass, pitched roof line and coloured logo sails. The complex was completed in 1988, and the architects were Fitzroy Robinson. The firm specialises in such retail centres: the Treaty Centre, Hounslow; the Trocadero, Piccadilly; the Broadway, Bexley Heath, for instance. Surrey Quays strives to be a cheerful and positive place; two murals hang above the entrances., perhaps not noticed that much by the shoppers scurrying in for their week's provisions, but they record the area's shipping heritage, and its artistic recreation; there are nautical motives: portholes, railings, life buoys. At the southern entrance there is a branch of Clinton card shops, and opposite a branch of Tesco's with its superabundance of packaged stuff, and large blown up historical photographs at the 29 checkout points. Most appear too in book form: in the majestic compilation *Dockland life: a pictorial history of London's docks 1860-1970,* Mainstream Publishing 1991. The shops are almost exclusively branches of well known chains, but in the central promenade area small traders have their stalls, selling potted plants, crazy balloons, dolls, fashion accessories, candles and fragrances. The central area is the climax of excitement: two dolphins, fountains, with reflecting mirrors on an escalator, a staircase, and a lift in a golden, red domed, glass cage. Ships' masts with flag streamers rise out of the lift shaft, and adjacent to *Burger King* the excitement reaches to its peak with a kiddies play paradise called *Discovery Planet*: slides, tunnels, all designed by fitness experts and brought in from America. An even larger one is located at Clapham Junction. It is owned by Burger King who can lay on special parties with goodie bags. In this central area you find clothes shops, *Holland and Barrett* health foods, a sports shop *Sports Division*, branches of *Dolland & Aitchison*, opticians, *Thomas Cook* and estate agents. *BHS* have a large clothes store at the northern end of the centre with show case windows.

I was there one evening, and found that it was getting time to eat once again. I sat in the shelter near the *Canada Water windmill* (see Southwark & Bermondsey News, August 19th, 1991) and munched my Tesco cheese and onion puff pastry and drank my Jamaican grapefruit crust called Ting, and watched the activity in the large car park forecourt: saw yuppies from the 1980's, all alone, hair cut short, walking very upright, carrying their computers home; saw funny kids on bicycles, fat Mediterranean ladies munching crisps, a schoolboy kicking an empty booze can with the utmost concentration: all people lost in their own worlds. As darkness came down I made my way northwards: called in at the *Canada Estate Tenants Hall* to inspect the striking new mural by George Baker, alerted to its existence through an article in Southwark News, June 5th, 1997. Barry Duckett, chairman of the association since 1992 told me of a community of dock workers, whose members have moved away by now or otherwise were dead, killed not infrequently by the hardness of the labour, labour you had to do without question if you wanted to eat. On to the Time and Talents Community Centre to listen to Fred Sage, former stevedore under contract to the National Dock Labour Board and recent founder of tour guides associations in Southwark, Greenwich and Deptford. Bow-tied Stuart Rankin, railway and maritime historian opened and closed the evening: a mixed gathering of interested young and old people. Fred gave us history, wanted us to be proud of where we were living, clicked his slides in and out and spoke of his love-hate relationship with a trade which had killed his father so early; spoke of his appearance as witness at the Old Bailey, and his fond memories of Lower Road and its bouncing pub pianos.

Above: *Mural at northern (BHS store) entrance to Surrey Quays Shopping Centre*. This dramatic, brilliantly coloured composition, executed by Murals and Banners celebrates and records Surrey Dock's importance as a centre for the timber and grain trades.

Above: *Former dock offices*, built 1892, Surrey Quays Road; now used by a variety of organisations and small businesses: two wings lie behind the facade on either side of a small garden. The South London Gallery holds a watercolour of this subject by Dorothy Mills.

Above: *Deal porters sculpture*, Canada Water (facing Deal Porters Way), by Philip Bews (based on photograph in old training manual). The blue arc is intended to suggest a boat.

Above: *L.C.C. flat, Redriff Estate, Rotherhithe*: a wood engraving by Rachel Reckitt (published in 'London South of the River', by Sam Price Myers, Paul Elek, 1949). An interesting interior; a cat lies on a rug between the two indolent, dreaming men.

Above: *The mural in the southern entrance to Surrey Quays shopping centre*, executed by Murals and Banners. An outstanding trompe l'oeil type mural commenting on a community 'reinventing' its past for decorative and educational purposes.

# IS THIS THE NEXT CENTURY?
## New housing, schools and a church around the shopping centre

The shopping centre experience is one of brightness, of happy acquisition, of material plenitude; but if you stray away behind Canada Water, you are at once engulfed in an alien, almost extra-terrestrial landscape of silence and stillness. Architects, the best ones, are visionaries, are in the business of staring into the future, yet aware too of the present; like composers they hope their creations will survive, will be around for many years hence. A perambulation of Canada Street, Needleman Street with the Albion channel running between (from Canada Water to Surrey Water), and environs may give us more than a hint of things to come. In *Canada Street* a new station of the Jubilee Line is to open soon: we spot the glass, metal topped drum entrance, with a new bus station adjacent. Opposite the station new properties are currently in progress; the northern firm Persimmon Homes is engaged on a project of 104 apartments: the sales brochure depicts an attractive layout of blocks with varying roof structures built around an ornamental garden courtyard, blocks named after trees. *Needleman Street* is dominated by *Hithe Point*, another development from Barratt's: gigantic sloping gables, a diversity of windows, and wide open courtyards. Basque Court opposite, by way of contrast is a long, barrack like red brick development: from CZWG architects, built in 1993 for the Crystal Palace Family Housing Association.

At night time the landscape comes into its own: lights gleaming everywhere, in the background the brooding angular shapes of *Harmsworth Quays*, the printing works of the Daily Mail, the Mail on Sunday and the Evening Standard, opened by Mrs Thatcher in 1989; and people invariably all alone: coming home overloaded with work worries, or with shopping bags, or getting out for a run around. It seems to be housing, housing, and more housing; the TV set, the telephone, the fax machine, the internet the only life lines perhaps; or else gazing at the vast, empty sky, contemplating what might lie beyond it.

*Wolfe Crescent*, off Canada street is another architectural extravaganza from CZWG for Lovell Urban Renewal, built in 1989, and again our imagination is stimulated and teased. The semi circular crescent has curious, wavy, almost curtain like borders to the garage entrances (suggesting perhaps the love the owners bestow on their machine?). The four octagonal blocks with their green, sliced off domes overlook the canal and have been given hard sounding English names: Gorham, Monkton, James, Carlton Houses. They are curious structures with their triangular shaped balconies and porthole windows; but even more curious is the block at Saunders Close which stands alone in isolation outside the crescent.

We live in an age when new buildings are never quite what they seem. Is this a kind of perversity, or is it a sense of many possible future uses? Could the octagons turn into an observatory? Could the *Alfred Salter Primary School* become something else? When first encountered, this highly successful new school, opened in October 1995, suggests perhaps a sports stadium. Behind, in fact, there are extensive community sports facilities and a nature garden. A long exhibition gallery runs along the top of the building with smaller wings behind. The entrance foyer is very spacious and light with exhibition shown cases, and the sensitive portraits of Alfred Salter, wife Ada, and daughter Joyce, painted by South East London artist Ayshe Price. The portraits were painted for the South London Mission at the suggestion of John Beasley and are on loan to the school. The artist has a religious background, is a helper and inspirer of people, and has made many portraits of people who have passed away.

What is one to make of the new Roman Catholic church close by in St Elmos Road, *Our Lady of the immaculate Conception*? - built in 1987, architects: Gerald Murphy, Burles, Newton and Partners, with its slanting roof structures, its lancet windows tucked away in corners (stained glass made by a monk from Buckfast Abbey), its narrow entrance way. The church community is thriving and has close links with the new primary school next door. Father Ellis lives above the church. Father John Clark (former priest here) was profiled in Southwark News, January 26th, 1995. *St John's Primary School*, 1990, architects: Chambers, Goodwin and Partners suggests at first a laboratory complex, yet it too is successful and thriving and an article in Southwark News, September, 26th, 1996 recorded its fifth anniversary celebrations. *Redriff Primary School* lies to the east, off Salter Road, and is a much older establishment. Its earlier 1910 LCC building was at the bottom of Rotherhithe Street. The present day 1990 building has cream and grey brickwork, blue and red painted structures and feels friendly and intimate. In the entrance you can see the tug-boat sculpture made by Peter McLean and pupils in 1990.

*Bacon's College* in Timber Pond Road certainly suggests externally a high tech business park, and in fact the school was designed as a show piece City Technology College, run by trustees and directly influenced by the last Tory government, and all the latest technology dominates the school and its thinking. Southwark News celebrated its first two years in its issue of October 7th, 1993, with a four page feature including a long interview with the then principal Peter Jenkins (the principal today is Clive Grimwood).

Beyond, accessed by a short steep path, lies *Stave Hill*, a fitting place of climax for any first time visitor; the steps to the top face Dock Hill Avenue. Engulfed in trees and lamps this vista over towards the City, with Tower Hamlets to the east (the river is not visible from this point), was used by LDDC for the cover of its booklet on regenerated Surrey Docks. Up here on Stave Hill it seems as if the mood below has evaporated almost instantaneously, and we are now engulfed in something altogether more optimistic and confident as we sense the sheer scale of the metropolis and the prodigious human effort that has brought it all into being.

Back at ground level, however, it is not euphoria, not uncertainty, but dismay which we experience when we encounter the seven white warehouse sheds forming what is being marketed as the *Canada Water Retail Park* (105,00 square feet of development from PSIT). The buildings are completed, yet at present totally empty; there are huge car parking areas, lighting has been installed, there are rows of squat bollards, and seat here and there, but nobody and nothing at all else is there. At the time of writing it seems like a coda of resounding emptiness to a century now ending.

Opposite: *A bas relief of Surrey Commercial Docks* at top of Stave Hill (culminating point of Dock Hill Avenue), sculpted by Michael Rizzello: a point of reference for the surrounding redeveloped area.

Opposite: *The new Alfred Salter Primary School, Archangel Street.* The tree logo suggests new life. Building designed by London Borough of Southwark Council.

154

# DOCKLANDSCAPE REINVENTED: into Greenland and South Docks

Oh yes, the cynical visitor might declare: all this came out of the architect's doodle pad: grids, and curves and circles repeated over and over again, as the architect sat through some interminable, exasperating meeting. One must bear in mind of course, the landscape which it replaces: empty sheds and general abandonment and desolation. Today, some seven years on after many of the buildings were completed, the place looks as if it is settling down to become a quiet, yet highly distinctive residential area, enjoyed when they are there by those who can afford the thousands and thousands of pounds they must give in return. The housing at *Brunswick and Greenland Quays* is protected by two screens of trees and ground level arcading; behind the dockside facades there are attractive courts with more trees, garages and narrow passage ways. The developer was Daniel Homes. The warm, brown brickwork conveys a private, yet contented domesticity. At Greenland Quays balconies and window frames are painted red and green.

To the south, the main landmark is *Baltic Quay* with a fourteen storey tower, striking one with its brilliant yellow frames and blue glass and concrete columns; designed by Lister Drew Haines for the developers Skillion, it is currently being marketed for residential use, but it suggests rather a conference centre: a place swarming with retail managers, property agents, technocrats, political party officials. With its noise and aggression it renders almost invisible the small 1902 dock office building at Swedish gate. In front of Baltic Quay there are the two blocks, built around courtyards of *Swedish Quays*; designed by Price and Cullen for Roger Malcolm Ltd, the mood here is quite different: the small window panels in varying patterns up to roof level create a sense of studious concentration; there is much attention to detail, from balcony decoration to drainpipes. When I spoke to David Price on the telephone he acknowledged the influence of late nineteenth century arts and crafts architects such as Voysey. The thin columns at ground floor level give the whole site, however, a certain kind of precariousness and uncertainty, which is felt more keenly across the water at *Finland Quay*. Here there are seven, identical blocks of residences, designed by Richard Reid for Lovell Urban Renewal, conveying a mood of caution and a curious sense that these cut-out facades could be taken apart and reassembled.

You find another, less prestigious project designed by David Price at *Helsinki Square*, beyond Finland Quay: two large blocks with eight smaller ones at dockside: a project for the South London Family Housing Association.

The *water sports centre* lies to the east of the filled in entrance to the Grand Surrey Canal. This shedlike building with blue doors and frames is a centre for watersports courses and activities, it runs fitness sessions, has bar and catering facilities and function rooms. It opened in 1990, with over £1.2 million funding from LDDC. To the west of the old canal entrance you encounter a capstan and a jigger (for opening and closing of local gates); confronting us like museum pieces on their stands.

More community facilities are to be found on the north side of Greenland Dock, beyond the entrance to Russia Dock woodland: at *Russell Place,* dominated by the tall block Tavistock Tower you will find shops and a pub the *Moby Dick* grouped around a square. The dockside facade is given distinction with its flight of steps, the three green painted metal canopies, and the brick planters.

*Queen of Denmark Court* and *Princes Court* lie beyond South Sea Street on either side of the dock entrance: a rather soulless induction to the vastness of the dock beyond. Garden areas both communal and private with ground level fencing and trellises lie within. One is struck by a certain degree of fussy detail and a bland, depressing, institutional kind of overall design. What do the residents feel as they look out through their windows, across to the Isle of Dogs, or down at the boarded up lock keepers office, and the tiny tide gauge house, and William Pye's 'Curlicue'? A sense of quite profound boredom, I guess. More stimulation can be had at the swing bridge (guarded over by a splendid old lamp) and the observation platform beyond, with their interesting LDDC interpretation panels. There is a 1796 water-colour drawing in reproduction of the mansion at the far end of the old Howland Dock, just before its demolition, and you can read about Elizabeth Howland and her marriage to the future 2nd Duke of Bedford in 1695. Down below, you will see solitary runners and cyclists, driven to keep fit fanaticism perhaps through an overwhelming desire for stimulation in a place where perhaps it is hard to have a sense of belonging, hard to establish links with any kind of community.

*'Privileged ice': unloading ice for the hospital only, despite the General Strike at Surrey Commercial Docks;* a drawing by H.W. Koekkoek from the Illustrated London News, August 12th, 1911. An interesting study of human, animal and mechanical power, with an unusual cargo.

Above: *Bust sculpted by Michael Rizzello* at Brunswick Quay (north east corner of Greenland Dock); unveiled March 28th, 1990 by Professor Peter Scott (president of the Institute of Civil Engineers).

Above: *The old Tide Gauge,* Greenland Passage. Note the LDDC circular plaque.

Above: *Hydraulic capstan,* Greenland Passage; turned by high pressure water it helped ships in and out of the dock. 'Curlicue' lies beyond.

Above: 'Curlicue' *by William Pye* at Greenland Passage. A curious, ambiguous structure.

The *South Dock* overflows with moored boats. It is London's largest working marina and has berths for some 200 vessels. A floating pub is here too: the Wibbley Wobbley is an old German cruiser, converted to a pub some 8 years ago (article in South London Press, July 15th, 1997). To the south there is a long housing development, with many fussy strips of brown brick, and with yellow balconies. Close to the dock entrance one discovers the *lock control building*, designed by Conran Roche. Its pleasing blend of granite and glass, circular central window, railings and flat roof suggest an architect's house, rather than a functional structure. Indeed, many new buildings may well be designed with an uncertainty of possible uses in mind. Behind is a brand new residential block just completed: *Dockmasters House*, a Galliard Road Homes development, designed by James Urquhart (of BUJ Architects in Mill Street, responsible for a variety of other projects in Limehouse, Wapping and the Isle of Dogs). It has a dramatic, and surprising presence tucked away in this far corner. The houses are protected with unusual, fortress like structures, and have precipitous staircases to upper storey entrances; sandwiched between high rising blank walls they inspire an almost vertiginous dread. The southern side, by way of complete contrast, has double tiered balconies made of Canadian redwood, of startling theatricality. I phoned the architect the next day and he agreed that it was an unusual construction: a place where intruders could be watched and kept at bay.

Returning home from my tour of inspection of this new place, I was struck by the dream-like, almost surreal quality of the whole development; the capricious, dissolving cloudscape reminded me of the extraordinary ceiling painting I had discovered earlier that afternoon at St Crispin's Church, Southwark Park Road; and the eerie silence, the forest of boat mastings clinking away monotonously, with almost Beethovenian insistence, in the wind, and the scattered relics of a working dock, all brought to mind quite forcefully the compelling images of the artist Edward Wadsworth.

Above: *Ship & Whale pub, at number 2, Guliver Street* in the north eastern corner of Greenland Dock. The alley way to the right is Randalls Rents, a reference to Randalls ship building yard here in the eighteenth and early nineteenth century (commemorated by an LDDC plaque); Queen of Denmark Court (foundation stone laid by Prince Hendrik of Denmark, December 1988) can also be glimpsed.

Above: *A view of Greenland Dock,* showing the residential blocks Swedish Quays, and Baltic Quay, and the water sports centre.

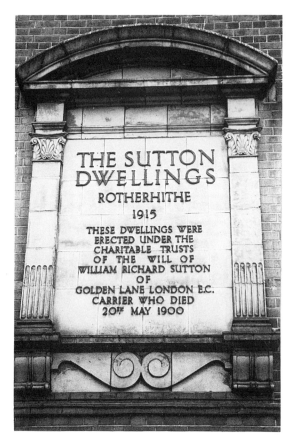

Above: *Sutton Dwellings;* a quiet, dignified estate off Plough Way. It makes a telling contrast with the post-modernist architecture around Greenland Dock.

Above: *The new mural by George Baker at the entrance to Canada Estate tenants association hall;* the artist's younger self is depicted on the left; a yellow propeller on the right; bottom panels show jubilee line construction work and scenes from the two older tunnels.

# IS THIS URBAN TRANQUILLITY? - into the lakes and woods

After the head-splitting sensation of Wolfe Crescent, a development, equally extraordinary, called *The Lakes* in part of the old Norway Dock, just behind FinlandQuay West at the eastern end of Greenland Dock comes as a soothing discovery. The complex which can be entered through a number of entrances, consists of a multitude of attractive small houses built over the central lake, surrounded, protected lovingly by larger blocks, terraces and crescents. There is an inner crescent, surrounded by water, with a fountain on one side. This is an early 1990's development by Ideal Homes, architects: Shepheard, Epstein and Hunter (architects of Wapping Sports Centre, and Pelican Wharf, Wapping Wall). It seems likely that the development was conceived as a kind of urban dreamland, something more soothing and intimate than the vast, chilly, empty space of Greenland Dock nearby which at night-time especially seems to swallow you up, such is its size; and not as decadent feeling as Shadwell Basin. Swans and water fowl are at the Lakes, but there is still a sense of unease at the strangeness of it all. These are immeasurably expensive properties and here as in other strictly private residential complexes, the penetration of this community would seem a virtual impossibility, as indeed it may seem to the residents themselves.


*Russia Dock Woodland* covers an area of some 34.5 acres and came into being in 1980. It lies just to the west of the Lakes and is accessed at its southern most end by a foot tunnel under Redriff Road. We can wander around here in this pleasant, natural feeling locality, thinking perhaps about nothing; but this is a place to study nature and Southwark council's Parks Ranger Service has issued a very attractive nature trail which guides you along the old quay side of the Grand Surrey Canal, to Stave Hill and the adjacent ecological park, past the southern end of the sports ground, onto Globe Pond and its stream and top pond leading to Salter Road with the Lavender Pond Nature Park beyond. Many trees, plants and wildlife are pointed out to you. There are bridges to linger on, and tall backed metal seats to rest on.

Above: Another work of art, an etching by Jen Parker, commissioned to commemorate the 375th anniversary of the sailing of the Mayflower. The first church is depicted and nature celebrates the departure with great joy: from top right to top left the artist has depicted: thrush, swallow, thistle, robin, daffodil, shamrock, rose, peacock butterfly, char, cod, mackerel, May blossom, sea horse, black seabass, rainbow trout, summer flounder, monarch butterfly, bloodroot, false spikenard, liver leaf, wake robin, black eyed Susan, mocking bird, Jack in the pulpit, cardinal, bald headed eagle.

161

# ENVOI

Everywhere, always, there is one thing you can never forget: and that is time: time past, present and future; the frame of the world is most certainly constantly passing away; we cannot seize the moment; we are too distracted today, too bewildered, too overloaded with data and images; we are the distracted, lost ones of the century, wandering in a landscape of many constructions, deconstructions and reconstructions; a society which is so entangled in its multi-ethnicity, that we may well doubt whether we have any identity at all.

Think globally, act locally, say the pundits; yet what is locality? Where is community? The highly paid professionals, returning home late in the evenings all alone, the small business people and thrusting entrepreneurs, the underclass people, artists, writers, all pursue their different ends, do not seem to belong to one another. Confusion, bafflement, fragmentation prevail. And what of the globe? Has the world now shrunk to the size of a yellow tennis ball we can hold in the palm of our hand?

Resplendent marble foyers, buildings which look as if they are tumbling down, or just going up, buildings turned inside out...a gigantic new Tower of Babel dominates the landscape today; what does the flashing light up there wish to communicate? imminent disaster? psychedelic excitement? the arrival of the space age?

Moons, planets, astral bodies will no doubt appear in the iconography of the future; the sale of telescopes will boom; astronomy will become a cult pursuit; unearthly stillness, vast empty space, and machines pulsating away with their own, man made, man fed mechanical lives; all this, no doubt, will feature in the landscape of the future, of tomorrow...Let us hope that it will all not be too bad; let us hope that we will be able to go on living.

Yet, it is possible that nothing at all changes; that we remain for ever as we were when we became newly emerged adults; our emotional web as then still sustains us; then, as now, and forever, perhaps, a sense of colossal expectation, and untold dread...

*Peter Marcan, Bermondsey, 1997.*

Over: *The World War II section from the mural at the Dockers' Call-on Shelter, Redriff Road;* designed by Jane Colling, in collaboration with members of the Bermondsey Artists Group, and completed in October 1993. Adjacent sections depict the 1920's, 1950's and 1970's.

# NOTES ON ARTISTS FEATURED

**ANGEL, R.J.** Engineer and surveyor to the old Bermondsey Borough Council. His pen and ink drawings made during the first two decades of the century record many now vanished buildings. His work is held by Southwark Local Studies Library and has been reproduced in the Bermondsey borough council guide books, its catalogue of prints and drawings, and Beck's History of Rotherhithe, 1907.

**APPLETON, Geoffrey.** Professional graphic artist, currently living near Leek, Staffordshire.

**BAKER, George.** George Baker lives on the Canada Estate, Rotherhithe. Aged seventy, he is just starting out in creative art, and has been studying at Southwark College. In his previous life he was a tug skipper and pilot, ran pubs, and travelled the world. Articles celebrating the Canada Estate Tenants Association hall mural appeared in Southwark News, June 5th, 1997 and Jubilee Express (Jubilee Line magazine), summer 1997.

**BERMONDSEY ARTISTS' GROUP.** Ron Henocq, director of the Cafe Gallery, Southwark Park has contributed the following: This 40 strong group of artists working in a variety of media and styles was founded in 1983 and held an inaugural exhibition in the Chapter House of Southwark Cathedral. The membership comes from a wide range of cultural and racial backgrounds and is open to artists living or working in the London Borough of Southwark. The elected Council of Management of the Bermondsey Artists' Group runs the Cafe Gallery in Southwark Park which shows a mixed programme of exhibitions which includes shows resulting from projects with local children and various community groups. There is an annual Open Exhibition which is entirely open to all to exhibit. The Bermondsey Artists' Group also organises workshops for children and intends to extend this aspect of its work by building a special community education room at the gallery.

**BEWS, Philip.** Born 1951, he studied landscape architecture at Manchester Polytechnic and later fine art at Liverpool Polytechnic. Between 1974 and 1982 he was an associate landscape architect with Runcorn New Town Development Corporation. Between 1986 and 1988 he was sculptor in residence at Birchwood School, Warrington and he published an illustrated booklet on this residency. Since 1993 he has been an advisor on visual arts to the North West Arts Board. Deal Porters, 189-990, and the pigs and donkey, 1992 at Barnards Wharf are the only pieces of his in London. Other 1990's projects include 'Time and Tide', a 1993 commission for HM Customs and Excise HQ, Queens Dock, Liverpool, collaboration with Diane Gorvin; 'Ymir', a large Portland stone carving for the Garden of the Blind, Grosvenor Park, Chester, commissioned 1994 by the Chester Civic Trust; 'Queen of Mercia', 1994 for Halton Borough Council and Manchester Ship Canal Company; and 'Mill girl and calf' for Charter Walk Shopping Centre, Burnley, in collaboration with Diane Gorvin. From 1986 onwards he has staged some 20 large scale public fire sculpture events in the North West and East Anglia. He now lives in Coalway, near Coleford, Gloucestershire.

**BLOXAM, Joan Mary.** Landscape artist, black and white artist, miniaturist, lithographer and art teacher active in the first three decades of the century. She exhibited with a variety of societies and had a solo show at the Walker Gallery, Bond St. Southwark Local Studies Library and the Lambeth Archives hold a small number of her drawings. The Atheneum Press published her book *Walks around London* in 1937. Her work was on the market recently: print dealer Elizabeth Harvey Lee's catalogue number 14 featured two watch house subjects; at Waterloo Bridge Road and at Bow Church, East London.

**CECIL, Rose.** Lady Rose, artist and photographer is a member of the great English family the Cecil's of Hatfield House. She was living at Corbetts Wharf, Bermondsey Wall East in the mid 1980's and she made a range of pictures of dockland subjects, including demolition scenes. Her Victoria Royal Dock oil painting is reproduced in *A London Docklands Album* (Peter Marcan Publications, 1992). However, she is in no way London focused and since 1978 has travelled widely: around the world in 1980-1, thirteen months, and most recently a three month painting expedition in the Galapagos Islands. In 1989 and 1990 she was in Tibet, China and Nepal. She is naturally talented and creates appealing and unusual work from any subject matter which attracts her. Her portraits are especially sensitive. She has had solo exhibitions at the Parkin Gallery and the Rebecca Hossack Gallery.

**CHASE, Peter.** Peter Chase's atmospheric, nostalgic coloured etchings of London riverside and dockland subjects date from the mid 1980's, an enterprise instigated by East End art dealer Andrew Lamont. Both sides of the river are frequently depicted: *Limehouse Lady; 'Them Good old days', An old-fashioned look; Evening light, Rotherhithe; Wapping Wharf; Old and new, Isle of Dogs* (reproduced in *A London Docklands Album*). Other London subject matter has included Thames bridges, Battersea Power Station and St Paul's Cathedral. More recent projects have included a series of drawings on crystalline minerals at the Natural History Museum, and a series on puppets. He has now retired from his teaching post at Bournemouth and Poole College of Art & Design. He is a committee member of the Printmakers Council.

**COLLING, Jane.** A member of the Bermondsey Artists' Group she designed the dockers call on shelter mural in Redriff Road. She currently works for an animation film company. Screen printing is a speciality, and she is working on an A-Z sequence of prints (everything in each print begins with a certain letter).

**DONLIN, Martin**. Born in 1959 in Hockley, Essex, and now resident in Wimborne Minster, Dorset, the artist studied architectural glass 1984-87 in Swansea and since 1988 has worked on numerous etched and stained glass commissions for public buildings. Other London commissions include work for the Broadgate Club, and the Espee Club. 1997 commissions have included an enamelled glass wall for the Harbour Lights Cinema, Southampton, and a stained glass screen for West Dorset General Hospital, Dorchester.

**FEIBUSCH, Hans.** Born in Frankfurt-am-Main in 1898, he came to London in 1930 where he quickly acquired recognition; his career as a painter of outstanding religious murals for churches began with a commission in 1937 from Edward D. Mills for Collier's Wood New Methodist Hall, London SW19. In the post-war years he worked with the architect Thomas F. Ford on many churches in the Southwark diocese, mainly scenes from the life of Christ at: St John's, Waterloo; St James', Merton; All Saints, Plumstead; St Barnabas, Eltham; All Hallows, Union Street, SE1 (now 'walled up'); Christ Church and St Stephen, Battersea, SW11; Saint Crispins, Southwark Park Road and Holy Trinity, Rotherhithe. Central London work includes: St Vedast's, EC2; St Alban The Martyr, Holborn. There are two recent publications: *Hans Feibusch, the heat of vision*, edited by David Coke, Lund Humphries Publishers for Pallant House Gallery Trust, Chichester, 1995; and *Feibusch murals: Chichester and beyond* published by Chichester Institute of Higher Education, 1997.

**FLANDERS, Dennis.** (1915-1994). Well known, prolific topographical and architectural artist, working in black and white, and water-colour. He was a 'special' artist on the Illustrated London News from 1956 to 1964, and also worked for the Yorkshire Post, the Birmingham Post, the Sunday Times and the Daily Telegraph. They published his first drawing in 1937 of Trafalgar Tavern, Greenwich. He was made a freeman of the Painter-Stainers' Company in 1966. His first book of published drawings were the 18 drawings he contributed to *Chelsea: from the Five Fields to the World's End*, by Richard Edmonds, Phene Press, 1956. In 1974 Charles Skilton published his *The great livery companies of the City of London*; and in 1984 the Oriel Press published his majestic collection of 224 drawings covering the country: *Britannia*: being a selection from the work of Dennis Flanders...landscape and architecture of the British Isles. He has not drawn much in the docklands areas. The Guildhall Library has a large collection of his work and mounted an exhibition in 1986.

**FRIED, David George.** His pen and ink drawings reproduced in this publication were especially commissioned as were those in the companion volume *Visions of Southwark*. His biographical details are given in *An East London Album* (Peter Marcan Publications 1992) which reproduces two of his works. He is particularly sensitive to the decadence of inner city life, and his drawings of small, bewildered figures dwarfed by strange relics from the past make a telling comment on our society which often seems at the end of its history. He lived in the Shoreditch/Hoxton area for some 12 years, and recently moved to Stoke Newington. He continues to work part-time as an art therapist. A one-man exhibition is currently under consideration.

**GABAIN, Ethel.** (1883-1950). Distinguished, but little known lithographer, the wife of the very original print-maker John Copley. Most of her 300 odd lithographs up to the early 1930's are of adolescent and young women in intimate interior settings, as well as a series on the French pantomime character Pierrot. Her prints executed as an official war artist in the 1940's form a vivid and technically accomplished record of war time work and activity. The Ministry of Information published two sets of her lithographs: Children in wartime; and Women's work in the war. Catalogue number 34, 1985, from the print dealers Garton and Cooke is a useful survey of the two artists' output.

**GORVIN, Diana.** Born in 1956, she studied at Bournemouth & Poole College of Art. She was employed as a sculptor by Warrington & Runcorn Development Corporation 1982-6 and her work there is described and illustrated in their booklet *Sculpture in the new town*. In 1996 she was artist in residence at the Midland College, Perth, Australia. Dr Salter's daydream, 1990; and the geese and donkey, 1992, bronzes at Barnard Wharf are her only pieces to be seen in London. Other pieces of the 1990's include gates and wrought iron panels. She often works in collaboration with her partner Philip Bews. They have now moved from the North West and live in Coalway, near Coleford, Gloucestershire.

**HASSELDINE, Ernest.** Illustrator associated with the South London Mission, his drawings appear in their annual reports of the early 1920's, in Walter Spencer's account of the mission *The glory in the garret*, published in 1932 by the Epworth Press, and in *Ballads of Bermondsey*, by Leslie Davison, published in 1943 also by the Epworth Press.

**HUXLEY, Jonathan.** (b.1965). Figurative painter; currently living in Lee Green, London SE12. Studied at the Royal Academy School 1989-92; exhibits at the Coombes Contemporary and Crane Kalman art galleries. In 1995 executed a historical (rope works) mural for Bristol City Council.

**ISON, Leonora.** With Walter Ison wrote *English church architecture through the ages*, Barker, 1972. Guildhall Library has a pen and ink drawing by her of St Margaret Pattens, dated 1935.

**JANES, Norman Thomas.** (1892-1980). Landscape artist, working in water-colour, etching, and wood engraving, he taught at Hornsey school of Art, 1928-60, and the Slade 1936-50. He was attracted to coastal, and riverside subject matter, often with boats, and two further examples of his work are reproduced in *Artists and the East End* (Peter Marcan Publications, 1986).

**JARVIS, Don.** (b.1936). Ever since studying painting at Camberwell School of Art in the 1950's, Don Jarvis has been especially interested in London riverside subject matter. He was especially active in Rotherhithe 1975-1985, producing many paintings and drawings of the locality, and in 1979 he issued two booklets of drawings: *Souvenir of Rotherhithe* Nos 1 and 2. His Aard Press has also issued booklets of his drawings of Hawksmoor churches, Canary Wharf, Tower Bridge, the river from Wandsworth to Woolwich - Riverline, with poems and his four novels. A retrospective of his paintings was shown in Minden, Germany in 1996. His oil painting *South Bank, Whitsun,* 1955 is reproduced in Geoff Hassell's *Camberwell School of Arts & Crafts: its students and teachers, 1943-1960.* This book also contains his reminiscences of his Camberwell years.

**JONES, Sydney Robert.** (1881-1966). Noteworthy for his carefully observed, detailed topographical work in many books published by The Studio, including his *London Triumphant,* 1941, and *Thames Triumphant,* 1943. He also contributed to the Sphere.

**KEMP, David.** Born in 1945 in the East End of London, he has lived in West Cornwall since 1972. He spent four years at sea before going to Wimbledon Art School. He has been making outdoor public sculpture since 1981 when he became one of the first resident sculptors at Grizedale Forest in Cumbria, and at the Yorkshire Sculpture Park. His extraordinary assemblages using materials ranging from bonze and welded steel to masonry and heavy timber have captivated and delighted the public: witty, yet disturbing comments on the industrial and technological culture of the nineteenth and twentieth centuries. His piece 'Vox populaire' (a 'Victorian voice-thrower') is in the reception area of the advertising agency Ogilvy and Mather at Cabot Square, Canary Wharf. His other pieces include: 'Heavy Plant', 20 feet high, a centrepiece at the new Sheffield Science Park; 'Old King Cole' is at Pelton Fell, County Durham made from colliery scrap and a recycled railway bridge; and the 'The old transformers', two Easter Island style heads overlooking the site of the former Consett steel works. More recently, following a disastrous arson attack on his workshop he has made costumes for a theatre project about pollution with the Cornish Kneehigh Theatre.

**KENNEDY, Colin.** Printmaker and member of the Bermondsey Artists' Group, currently living in Brighton. His coloured print 'Picnic in Southwark Park' depicts a figure in a balloon labelled B.A.G. snatching up a picnicker and his dog. It was used as the invitation card for the 1992 show.

**KOEKKOEK, H.W.** Simon Houfe comments (in his Dictionary of British book illustrators and caricaturists 1800-1914): 'presumably one of the large family of Dutch painters of this name'.

**KORNBLUTH, Nathaniel.** (1914-1997). The artist's atmospheric, yet topographically precise etchings and drawings of canal, dock and riverside scenes in London of the early 1930's enjoyed a revival of interest in the 1980's. In March 1986 he showed his complete etched work in the foyer of the Sir John Cass Art School, Whitechapel (next to the wholesale clothing business he managed and owned); his work was also exhibited at and sold through the Lamont Gallery, Bethnal Green; and his work reproduced and documented in *Artists and the East End* (Peter Marcan Publications, 1986), and in *A London Docklands Album.* His work is held by the Guildhall Library and elsewhere. He received instruction from Norman Janes, and it is interesting to contrast their two visions of the same subject: Cherry Garden Pier and adjacent warehouses (Norman Janes' etching used on cover of first edition).

**LOCKETT, David H.** Born in 1958, he studied at Bath Academy of Art and Westhill Teacher Training College. In 1987/88 he was teaching in Mozambique and currently teaches at the John Roan School in Blackheath. He has had one person shows at the Higherwater Gallery, Limehouse; at Lewisham Art House, and at Greenwich Theatre Art Gallery. His sweeping, composite paintings of urban and river and seascape have much drama. In the 1980's he published a book of drawings 'How we live, how we could live' in support of members of the National Union of Seamen.

**LORD, John Vernon.** (b.1939). A distinguished illustrator of children's books; most famous for his *The Giant Jam Sandwich* (how a village rid itself of a plague of wasps). He teaches illustration at Brighton University, and lives in Ditchling.

**MARCH, Sydney.** (1875-1968). One of the family of eight artistically talented children. He had a studio in Chelsea for a number of years and exhibited regularly at the Royal Academy. An early commission was a marble bust of Edward VII for Windsor Castle. Work by the March family is held at Bromley Museum, Orpington, and in 1995 an exhibition 'Cast in bronze: the works of the March family, sculptors of Locks Bottom' was staged there.

**McDONALD, Lesley.** Born in Luton, raised and educated in Surrey. Now married with two children, she still finds time to take as many and as varied photographs as possible. She is currently running a successful photography business.

**McLEAN, Peter.** Sculptor, educated at Cheetham's music school, Manchester and Reading University, he has been living and working in Rotherhithe/Bermondsey since the early 1970's. He was a founder member of the Bermondsey Artists' Group and often exhibits at their annual summer show. A year's residency at Redriff School culminated in the creation in 1990 of a tug boat sculpture standing at the entrance to the school. This led to the LDDC commission of the bronze sculpture at Cumberland Wharf. He writes of his piece: "In the early 1930's when 'Docklands' was a very different place, a young Rotherhithe lad reads his 'Sunbeam weekly' which has cast upon its pages the artist's version of the Mayflower story and beyond...the spirit of a 'Pilgrim father' appears behind the young lad and tuns the pages of the comic. He looks surprised, to say the least, at what the future holds. The old story of the Pilgrim's pocket is given a new twist. A bronze pocket has been fashioned into the pilgrim's coat and it has been said that any visitor from the New World who places a small object therein may find a new and more rewarding path in life. If all this sounds like a dream the presence of 'Bandit' the Staffordshire bull terrier rearing up on his hind legs soon brings you back to the present reality". Due to the considerable cost of casting, much of his work is in three-quarter relief, in wood and glass.

**MILLARD, Martin.** Freelance artist and illustrator, with special interest in black and white London topographical work. He has drawn extensively in South London and the East End. He has a degree in Fine Art from the School of Visual Art, New York City. He exhibits with the Nine Elms Group of artists (artists from Clapham, Vauxhall, and Battersea). The drawings reproduced in this publication were especially commissioned. In 1992 he issued a small booklet of drawings *Chelsea details*. He is also a trained lawyer.

**MILNE, Vincent.** Vincent Milne was born in Hackney in 1953. He studied at Goldsmith's College and the Royal Academy School. He currently has a studio at Chiserhale Studios, East London and lives in Deptford. He has always been preoccupied with London landscape, its river and canals and is currently recording the Millennium Dome site in North Greenwich. Other areas depicted include Canary Wharf, Surrey Quays and Butlers Wharf (both pre-development). Another mural, comparable to the Bermondsey Street project, also executed with Lynette Lombard, is located on the wall of the Zanzi bar pub, in Lambeth Road, overlooking the playground of St George's Primary School. He also teaches at a variety of London establishments (Mary Ward Centre, Blackheath Conservatory, Hampstead School of Art, etc.).

**MUMBERSON, Stephen.** Born in 1955, and educated at Brighton Polytechnic and the Royal College of Art, he is an artist of almost archetypal manic energy and productivity. His monumental series of over 70 linocuts made between 1991 and 1994 depicts many well-known buildings and sites in Central London. His pencil drawings of London subjects are equally impressive. He was elected a Fellow of the Royal Society of Painter-Engravers in 1995, and has taught at Middlesex University since 1987. Two further London linocuts are reproduced in the compiler's Visions of Southwark.

**MURALS AND BANNERS.** This is the enterprise of Carol Kenna and Stephen Lobb. They are based at the Greenwich Mural Workshop at the MacBean centre, MacBean Street, in Woolwich and work with a variety of clients, produce handbooks and carry out consultancy and educational work; they also design playgrounds, parks and gardens. Recent work includes the mosaic benches at the Rathmore Youth centre, Charlton. The 'Winds of Peace' (commissioned by GLC Peace Year, 1984) mural in Creek Road has now gone.

**PARKER, Jen.** An etching based around West Square, off St George's Road was published in the compiler's *Visions of Southwark*. She trained as an illustrator at Chelsea School of Art and for the last 14 years has been a full-time freelance illustrator and print-maker. Southwark Cathedral displays her large-scale pictorial map of the Southwark Diocese in the nave, and her impressive drawing commemorating the construction of the cathedral's new chapter house hangs at the entrance to the restaurant. Her commissions include work for special commemorations, and work for guide books published by Bessacarr prints (Doncaster).

**PELZ, Peter.** Other murals by the artist include: 'Caliban's Dream', rear of the National Theatre, Waterloo Road, a mural at the church of St Peter, Morden, and a triptych in Liverpool.

**PHILLIPS, Henry Laverock** (1834-1917). Worked for the South London Metropolitan gas works. Many of his drawings are based on earlier pictures and documents and Southwark Local Studies Library has two scrapbooks containing such material, plus two containing his press cuttings from the 1860's.

**PROUT, Victor.** Simon Houfe records (in his Dictionary of British Book Illustrators and caricaturists 1800-1914) simply that he worked as a water-colour painter, and was active 1888-1903.

**PYE, William.** (b.1938). An internationally acclaimed sculptor, best known to Londoners probably for his piece called Zemran outside the Queen Elizabeth Hall. His two water sculptures 'Slipstream' and 'Jetstream' at Gatwick Airport's new North Terminal received the Association of Business Sponsorship of the Arts Award in 1988 for the best commission of art in any medium. W.J. Strachan's book *Open air sculpture in Britain*, published by Zwemmer and the Tate in 1984 contains information on other public pieces. He had a studio at Surrey Docks in the 1970's.

**RIZZELLO, Michael.** Internationally famous sculptor, who works in most sculptural media and at all scales from large architectural works, public statuary to wild-life sculpture, portrait busts, plaques, medals and coin design. He has designed coins for some 90 countries. Work in the U.K. include the memorial to David Lloyd George in Cardiff, the portrait bust of Sir Thomas Beecham, Royal Opera House, Covent Garden; portraits of Reginald M. Phillips at the National Postal Museum, London, and Sussex University; statue of Sir William Sevenoke at Sevenoaks, Kent, a bronze fountain for Luton and Dunstable Hospital, aluminium sculptures for Sussex Square, London, and a portrait bust of Lord Stevens of Ludgate at Ludgate House. He was president of the Society of Portrait Sculptors 1968-73.

**ROMP, Oscar.** (b. 1963). Educated at Bretton Hall College and the Royal College of Art, Oscar Romp is a figurative, city life artist of great excitement and distinction. He has a studio in Camberwell. He works mainly on public art commissions in a variety of settings: hospitals, colleges, primary schools, prisons, old people homes, etc; his major project to date has been a series of thirty panels for a corridor at King's College Hospital, Denmark Hill entitled 'The Passage' (to find: go through Bessemer Road entrance, down main corridor, then turn left, past branch of W H Smith). This joyful, carefully observed evocation of hospital life, markets in Walworth and Brixton, and parkland (Ruskin Park) is a wonderful, uplifting experience and incorporates some 400 figures. In the concluding section there is a celebration of multi-cultural dance activity, and outgoing, exploratory energy (three cycling tableaux). He has written articles on this project for Artery (Arts for Health journal), issue 14, October 1996; and the Nursing Standard, July 31st, 1996. He is very keen on modern, freestyle dancing, and there is a series of drawings and paintings based on experiences in London night clubs. In 1998 he played the leading role in a short film 'Forgotten story' about a club dancer (made by Greenwich Films, director: Tom Tywhitt). The Museum of London acquired his charcoal drawing *Levi the jazz dancer* in 1997. His small output of distinguished prints (etchings and lithographs) includes: *Through the city lights*, 1989 (cyclist in deserted city street); *The hills are alive...and then the wind blew*, 1990 (motorway/storm scene); and *The demonstration*, 1992 (potato slicing machine). The Oxford Gallery (High Street, Oxford) has been stocking his prints. One of his first murals was in Hartlepool (commissioned by Gus Robinson Developments, with funding from Northern Arts), celebrating the town's past and present. Currently he shows his work at exhibitions organised by the London Arts Cafe (urban culture membership organisation), and at a variety of West End galleries.

**SARGEANT, James.** (b. 1954 in Boston, Lincolnshire). He worked with David Kindersley in Cambridge, 1981-6; then joined the building and restoration company Rattle & Kett Ltd; In 1989 formed a partnership company to design and supply decorative carving, sculpture and inscription; was involved with the restoration of St John's College Chapel, and the Sainsbury Wing of the National Gallery. Collaborated with Dhriwa Mistry RA on sculptural and design work at Victoria Square, Birmingham. Recent projects include: relief carving in brick at Otley College, Suffolk, and a copper tree fountain for Essex and Suffolk Water Company. Currently works for Norwich City Council designing street furniture, and is also working on the Great Court Project at the British Museum with Foster & Partners.

**SHEPHERD, Thomas Hosmer.** Son of George Shepherd, his delicate, precise water-colour topographical drawings have been long admired. Frederick Crace (his important collection is now in the British Museum) commissioned him to draw many threatened buildings, especially old taverns and almshouses. Five of his East End almshouse drawings are reproduced in *An East London Album* (Peter Marcan Publications, 1992).

**SOLOWAY, Louise.** Louise Soloway was born in London in 1962. She studied at Bath Academy and then from 1984-1987 was on a Commonwealth Scholarship to Baroda Faculty of Fine Arts. India. The brochure for her exhibition at the Jehangir Art Gallery, Bombay in 1986 contains a perceptive essay on her work by Rekha Rodwittiya. Returning to London she explored East End life in the Spitalfields area, and worked as artist in residence at Haggerston School, 1989-90; and Sandhurst Primary School, Lewisham, 1993; between 1990 and 1993 she was part time lecturer at Hackney 6th Form Centre. She had three solo shows in Tower Hamlets in 1987, 1989 and 1992. She specialises in bas-relief painted fibre glass works and has had commissions in the 1990's for such work from the London International Financial Futures Exchange, UBS Phillips and Drew, Oxford House Community Centre (photograph of this used as frontispiece to the compiler's *East London Album*), H.W. Fischer & Co, accountants, Salmon Brothers, Hong Kong, the new airport at Chek Lap Kok, Hong Kong and Smith Kline Beecham Pharmaceuticals. Since 1994 she has been a British Council artist in Hong Kong. Her work is characterised by an acute, yet humorous, and loving observation of diverse social activity and an outstanding technique which suggest that a remarkable career is unfolding. She has recently issued a colour brochure of her work.

**STEWART, James Lawson** Painter of picturesque old London subjects (often with Dickens' associations), active 1860's to 1880's. Work held by Guildhall Library, Museum of London, and Bishopsgate Institute. His 1887 water-colour of Jacob's Island, Bermondsey (held by the Museum of London) was reproduced as the frontispiece of the first edition of this publication.

**WASHINGTON, William.** (1885-1956). Oil painter and line engraver of architectural and figure subjects. He was the son of a railway signalman and taught at Southend, Clapham and Hammersmith art schools. Another demolition view is his etching The chamber of the House of Commons after the Blitz, 1941. His figure etchings include Clocks to Mend and the Cricket Bat Maker (reminiscent of the work of Stanley Anderson). The Guildhall Library, the British Museum and the V & A hold his work.

**WAY, Thomas Robert.** (1861-1913). Important artist in the revival of lithography in Britain, he helped Whistler and published a catalogue of his lithographs in 1896, and published a book on him in 1903. His own lithographs, mostly all London subjects, appear in the three collections *Reliques of Old London*, published by Bell 1896-1899, with text by H.B. Wheatley, and in *The Thames from Chelsea to the Nore*, text by Walter George Bell, published by John Lane/The Bodley Head in 1907, which includes views of London Bridge and Tower Bridge.

**WILLIAMS, Hubert.** (1905-1989). Studied at the Royal Academy Schools 1927-1932. He became a freelance artist drawing London architecture and street scenes, and his drawings were published in the Daily Chronicle, the Observer, The Times, and Blue Peter Magazine. He later undertook much portraiture and illustrated children's books. For the last twenty years of his life he lived in Cheltenham concentrating on portraiture and flower painting. His work is in a number of public collections including Westminster City Libraries, the South London Art Gallery, the Museum of London, and the Guildhall. His drawing of the Spa Road municipal buildings (before war damage) is used in a number of editions of the Bermondsey Official Guide. Some of his North Southwark drawings are reproduced in *Visions of Southwark*, (Peter Marcan Publications, 1997).

# ADVERTS

# OF RELATED INTEREST AND ALSO FROM PETER MARCAN PUBLICATIONS

*VISIONS OF SOUTHWARK*:  a collection of nineteenth and twentieth century pictures, photographs by Lesley McDonald, historical notes, and descriptive, imaginative writing.
ISBN: 1 871811 13 9.   174pp (232 illustrations).
This collection covers localities covered by the old London Boroughs of Southwark and Camberwell, extending from Bankside and London Bridge to Peckham, Nunhead and Camberwell.
The *newsletter, Autumn 1997 of the Southwark Heritage Association* comments: "You can travel these parts again, or even for the first time, with the affectionate eye and the fine phrases of the author".
..."a cracking read." *Southwark News, June 12th, 1997.*
..."graphic art and evocative writing combine to conjure up the quintessential atmosphere of this fascinating area of London." *Small Press Listings, Spring 1998.*
..."a quirky evocation of the borough area by area...a trove of information." *Camberwell Quarterly, November 1997.*

---

*A LONDON DOCKLANDS ALBUM*: a collection of nineteenth and twentieth century picture material from diverse sources.
Second revised impression (1996).
ISBN: 1 871811 12 0.  68pp (125 illustrations)
..."a fascinating collection of pictures." *East London Advertiser.*
..."a must for all collectors of East London memorabilia." *East London Record.*
..."each illustration is carefully captioned, making this much more than a picture book, giving it depth and value to anyone interested in the local history of the area." *Docklands News.*

---

*THE LORDS PRAYER IN BLACK AND WHITE, WITH DRAWINGS BY ARTHUR WRAGG.*
First published by Jonathan Cape in 1946, and now re-issued, to revive the name and work of a great English visionary graphic artist.
ISBN: 1 871811 01 5.  26pp.
..."strikingly original drawings." *Church Times*
..."the pictures are challenging to a fascinating extent". *Harry Williams, Community of the Resurrection, Mirfield.*
..."a magnificent booklet...Arthur Wragg's drawings are absolutely superb." *The Right Rev. Dr George Carey.*

---